Cries of Joy, Songs of Sorrow

Cries of Joy,

Chinese Pop Music

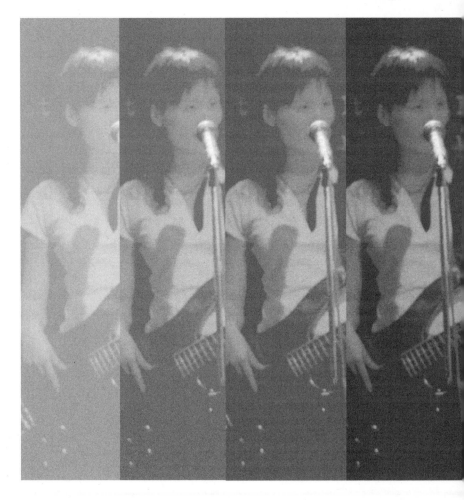

Songs of Sorrow

and Its Cultural Connotations

Marc L. Moskowitz

University of Hawai'i Press
Honolulu

15 14 13 12 11 10   6 5 4 3 2 1

Library of Congress Cataloging-in-Publication Data
Moskowitz, Marc L.
   Cries of joy, songs of sorrow : Chinese pop music and its cultural connotations /
Marc L. Moskowitz.
      p.   cm.
   Includes bibliographical references, discography, and index.
   ISBN 978-0-8248-3369-5 (hardcover : alk. paper)—ISBN 978-0-8248-3422-7
(pbk. : alk. paper)
   1. Popular music—China—History and criticism.   2. Popular music—Taiwan—
History and criticism.   3. Music—Social aspects—China.   I. Title.   II. Title:
Chinese pop music and its cultural connotations.
   ML3502.C5.M65 2010
   781.630951—dc22
                                        2009019774

An earlier version of chapter 5 was published as "Message in a Bottle: Lyrical Laments
and Emotional Expression in Mandopop," *The China Quarterly* 194 (2008): 365–379.
An earlier version of chapter 7 was published in *Popular Music* 28(1) (2009): 69–83.

Designed by University of Hawai'i Press Production Department
Printed by The Maple-Vail Book Manufacturing Group

For F. G. Bailey

Contents

Preface

One minute she's so happy / then she's crying on someone's knee /
saying laughing and crying / you know it's the same release.
—Joni Mitchell, "People's Parties"

This book draws on eighteen interviews in Shanghai and sixty-five interviews in Taipei with both laypeople and people working in Taiwan's music industry, including lyricists, performers, and people working in music companies. Because I was primarily interested in the presentation of, and reflection on, women's experiences in these songs, the majority of people I interviewed were women. Most of the people I interviewed were college educated urbanites in their twenties and early thirties. To protect the identities of those I interviewed, I often use their self-chosen English names. I have also drawn on a range of English and Chinese-language academic work and the popular press in the People's Republic of China (PRC), Taiwan, and the United States.

I should note in advance that, in opposition to some excellent commentary on an earlier draft of this book pointing out that not all of my readership will be from the United States, I have opted to continue to use the United States as a comparative point with China and Taiwan. I do so because of America's exceptionally strong influence on Mandopop and because those I interviewed often specifically referred to the United States to highlight their points on both music and culture. Although they often used the United States to mean "the West" as a general category, I am uncomfortable with using the term "Western" when using specific examples because of the tremendous range of music and cultures in Western nations and because it is too problematic on a number of ethical and intellectual levels.[1]

One of the greatest obstacles to this research has been the temporal popularity of songs and performers. As Stewart Ewen suggests for style, trying to present the latest trend is innately doomed in that "one of the main points of a style is that it will not remain current."[2] This was never more true than with Mandopop trends.

After several summers of updating the lyrics to reflect the most popular songs of that particular year, I finally gave up and replaced many of them with the songs I had begun this project with in the mid-1990s, because these were the songs that were mentioned most frequently in my interviews. Most of the songs that I cite from the mid-1990s have become classics. The newer songs that I discuss are so phenomenally popular that I can't imagine they will not be remembered years from now. Given the slow process of getting academic works published, however, even the newest of the songs in this book will seem out of date by the time this book is published. Thus, rather than attempting to present the latest trends or a comprehensive view of each artist who has been popular in the past twenty years, I focus on the central themes from the mid-1990s to today, using specific performers and songs as examples of general trends.

The songs that I discuss in the following chapters were either mentioned in interviews, taken from anthology CDs of "women's greatest hits" and "men's greatest hits," or had particularly strong sales. Because of limited space I only include one stanza of each song being examined. The complete Chinese lyrics, and my English translations for each song, can be found on my web page (http://people .cas.sc.edu/moskowitz/songs.html).

I confess to a certain frustration concerning the translations of the songs. Although I believe I have translated them accurately, the depth and expressiveness of feeling is lost both in rendering the poetic verses into English and in reading them without the accompanying melodies. Readers who are familiar with these songs may therefore want to hum the melodies while reading the lyrics—I have found that this helps.

The U.S. dollar amounts in this book are rounded-off sums from local currencies. For Taiwan I used a NT$34-to-US$1 conversion rate. For Hong Kong and the PRC I used a 7 Yuan/HK$7-to-US$1 conversion rate.

Acknowledgments

I would like to thank David K. Jordan for his careful and insightful readings of the initial manuscript and for his brilliant sense of humor, which kept me (relatively) sane through the darker periods of this project. Thanks also to Shuenn-Der Yu for being my patron saint in Taiwan and for being such a good friend over the years. Andrew Morris, David Schak, and Shuenn-Der Yu provided me with detailed and insightful feedback on an earlier draft of my manuscript. Jeffrey Bass, Elana Chipman, Terry Kleeman, Heather Levi, Scott Simon, and Jonathan Stock commented on particular chapters. Dr. Wu Jing-jyi provided a good deal of insight into Taiwan's culture with his characteristic flair. Patricia Crosby has continued to be the ideal editor, and I am grateful for her gentle but persistent nudging to make this book better. Special thanks to Bonnie Adrian and Thomas Gold, who served as anonymous external reviewers and who later agreed to reveal their identities so that I could give them their well-deserved acknowledgments by name. Their comments on the manuscript were some of the best I've ever received and have made this book far stronger than it otherwise would have been. My wife A-rey (Huei-jyun Jhang) deserves a medal of honor for her infinite patience with my tendency to hunch over the computer at all hours.

The Institute of Ethnology, Academia Sinica, was kind enough to offer me affiliation from May through December 2003 and from June 2005 through July 2006. The Fulbright Foundation was exceptionally generous in providing me with two consecutive grants to research and write on this project from July 2005 to May 2007. Because I draw on fieldnotes from previous research periods, I would also like to acknowledge the U.S. Department of Education Center for International Education for a Fulbright-Hays grant and the Chiang Ching-Kuo Foundation for their financial assistance during the late 1990s.

Anya Bernstein, in sharing some of her (and now my) favorite Taiwan pop, proved to me that Mandopop can, on occasion, have a humorous edge to it. Thanks also to Elaine Su (Su Qianyi) for being an endless fount of information on Taiwan's music. Reirei An (An Darui) helped me arrange interviews with Mandopop stars

I never would have met without her. I was also blessed with a spectacular group of research assistants who accumulated a range of written materials for me: Emily Blegen, Dianne Brizollara, Hanwen, and Amy Yu. My greatest thanks go out to those I have interviewed (you know who you are) who shared the intimate details of your lives with a frankness and thoughtfulness that I found both moving and inspiring.

Unless otherwise noted, the interviews were conducted in Chinese and all translations are my own. The mistakes in this book are also my own but, in the words of Douglas Adams, "Anything that is put down wrong here is, as far as I'm concerned, wrong for good."[3]

CHAPTER 1

The Tail Wags the Dog

Taiwan's Musical Counter-Invasion of China

> Heaven knows we need never be ashamed of our tears, for they are
> rain upon the blinding dust of the earth, overlying our hard hearts.
> —Charles Dickens, *Great Expectations*

For the most part, Americans who are familiar with Mandopop (Mandarin Chinese–language pop music) condemn it as vapid, uninspired, and somewhat painful to listen to. Yet by and large, people making these judgments either lack the linguistic skills to understand the sophisticated poetics of the lyrics or have not taken the time to do so. Mandopop has surprisingly complex cultural implications for such a seemingly superficial genre. It has introduced new gender roles to China, created a vocabulary to express individualism in direct contrast to state and Confucian prioritization of the group, and has introduced transnational culture to a country that had closed its doors to the world for twenty years. Mandopop songs are remarkably melancholy, but, as I hope to suggest with the opening quotes, its songs of sorrow can also be cries of joy, for their tearfulness reminds us of our humanity in a seemingly uncaring and increasingly commodified world.

Although this book focuses on Mandopop and its audiences in Shanghai and Taipei, this is really the tale of four cities—Beijing, Hong Kong, Shanghai, and Taipei. The Mandopop industry was born in the 1920s jazz era in Shanghai. It relocated to Hong Kong during China's civil war and spread to Taiwan in the 1970s. Hong Kong continues to have a thriving Mandopop industry, but Taiwan is the undisputed ruler of this terrain. The Mandopop industry seems to be slowly shifting back to Shanghai, its birthplace, but it seems safe to say that for the next decade, at least, Taiwan will maintain its Mandopop throne. Beijing, as the center of both state and musical masculinist nationalist discourse, can be heard shouting its condemnation of the music from the periphery.

There is already some excellent academic work on Chinese popular music, yet most of this scholarship concentrates on Beijing rock and for the most part

1

excludes Mandopop produced in Taiwan. This focus has more to do with the Peoples Republic of China's (hereafter PRC) economic and political might, and perhaps with Western academics' musical preferences, than with actual Chinese musical tastes, however. The reality is that Taiwan's Mandopop is far more popular in China than all of the music genres produced in the PRC combined. In 1992, Taiwan's music sales were already the third highest in Asia—after Japan and South Korea but ahead of much larger countries such as India and the PRC.[1] After Hong Kong's return to China in 1997, Taiwan took an even more central role in the PRC's imaginary, and from 2002 to today Taiwan's Mandopop has consistently accounted for approximately 80 percent of Chinese-language music sales in the PRC.[2]

It is nothing less than astounding that Taiwan, which houses 23 million people, can dictate the musical tastes of a nation of 1.3 billion. Taiwan is under the shadow of the PRC's economic, military, and political might, but, as will be evident in the following chapters, it dominates China's popular culture to such a degree that it is not surprising that the PRC government seems to worry that Taiwan is the proverbial tail wagging the PRC dog.

Indeed, it would be difficult to overemphasize the dramatic influence that Taiwan's pop culture has had on the PRC. Works of fiction by authors from Taiwan are extremely popular, the PRC's fashion industry closely emulates Taiwan, and Taiwanese-style restaurants and clubs in China are markers of status, conspicuous consumption, and participation in global culture.[3] The PRC music industry imitates Taiwan's musical and karaoke video styles,[4] and most of the songs on PRC-televised amateur singing contests today are from Taiwan. In Shanghai, Chinese radio has experienced a dramatic shift from the Beijing accent and focus on state matters to the softly spoken, fast-paced style of Taiwan radio,[5] and China's concerts, dancers, and advertising portray a world that looks and acts more Taiwanese than people in the PRC.[6] Indeed, walking down the streets of Shanghai today, one is accosted by the ubiquitous images of Taiwanese performers—posters of Jay Chou, Jolin Tsai, and Wang Lee-hom have long replaced Chairman Mao's portrait. Amateur singing contests, a constant on Shanghai's televised airways, inevitably feature Shanghaiese singing their favorite hits from Taiwan. In short, Taiwan's popular culture has saturated every corner of Chinese-speaking Asia in what many people in the PRC and Taiwan have called Taiwan's "counter-invasion of China."

Shanghai houses some 400,000 expatriate Taiwanese businessmen, and it dominates the Mandopop market, so in some sense it is no surprise to see Taiwan's imprint so visibly stamped onto the urban landscape of the PRC's economic center. Yet it marks changes of almost Twilight Zone proportions since my first visit to Shanghai in 1989.

In the following chapters I will explore a range of cultural connotations of

Taiwan-produced Mandopop in the PRC and Taiwan. While less threatening to the PRC state than the overt sexuality and celebration of consumerism that are expressed in U.S. pop, Taiwan has served to export a transnational musical ethos that is remarkably radical in comparison with the state-controlled music industry in the PRC. Taiwan has done much more than usher in a watered-down version of Western pop as is sometimes asserted. Rather, it has created a new musical ethos—a blend of traditional Chinese, Japanese, Taiwanese, and Western musical styles that has transformed into something new and delightful for Chinese-speaking audiences.

Taiwan's counter-invasion has had profound influences on PRC culture: It has (re) introduced images of women as emotional, gentle, and passive victims. It has also offered a wider range of male identities—though, as I will present in chapter two, this is a far more contested domain than mass-mediated women's roles. Mandopop has ushered in individualist ideologies and a globalized consumer culture, and it has provided a space to talk about human emotions such as loneliness and sorrow that have traditionally been highly discouraged by both the government and traditional cultural mores. Themes of urbanization, the shift to a capitalist infrastructure, the breakdown of traditional values, and an increasing sense of a social and moral vacuum all come into play with Mandopop.

There are of course other kinds of songs than those I am presenting here. In focusing on songs of sorrow I am examining a subset of one genre of music. Yet, as evinced by choices made in radio stations, karaoke, people's conversations, and CD sales, as well as magazine and television coverage (including music videos, the news, and television programming), it is clear that songs of sorrow remain by far the most prevalent form of Chinese-language music, and even people who are more interested in alternative music are extremely familiar with the more popular Mandopop songs.[7] Unlike the U.S. music industry, which has several distinctive musical forms (ranging from blues to country-western to pop), Mandopop is *the* Chinese-language musical genre in Taiwan, and all other musical styles, ranging from alternative to R&B to rock, are subsumed into this larger category. In the PRC there are other distinct musical genres—such as Beijing's rock movement, *xibeifeng*, revolutionary songs, and PRC pop music—but these all play a minute role in comparison with Mandopop from Taiwan.

Terminology for Contested Regional and Musical Identities

The divide between PRC pop on one end and Mandopop from Taiwan and Hong Kong on the other is so vast that the term "Gang-Tai pop"—popular music from Hong Kong (Xiang GANG) and Taiwan (TAIwan)—is used in both English language and PRC scholarship and mass media. The term is valuable in highlighting the fact that one is discussing PRC views of music produced outside its borders. Yet is also important to problematize this term, for "Gang-Tai pop" is all but meaningless to the people I interviewed in Taiwan who acknowledge that Hong Kong and Taiwan pop are quite similar when compared with PRC pop, but who also see the many distinctive qualities that separate Hong Kong and Taiwan, both culturally and musically. It is an especially problematic term in contemporary times when Malaysian, Singaporean, and American-born Chinese performers, to name a few, have become such central parts of the Mandopop industry. Yet in spite of my reservations, I have decided to continue using the term here. For one, most of these performers enter the market through music companies based in Taiwan. More importantly, the term Gang-Tai pop came up repeatedly in PRC scholarship, and exploring the striking divide between PRC pop and Gang-Tai pop is a central goal of this book.

To review, I will use the term "Mandopop" as a general category for Mandarin Chinese–language pop music, "Gang-Tai pop" when speaking of PRC perceptions of Mandopop from outside its borders, and specific regional categories (Hong Kong pop, PRC pop, and Taiwan pop) when appropriate. I will now explore the slippery issue of national identity in relation to Mandopop that has necessitated this care with terminology.

Flexible Personas, Shifting Regional Identities

As Jeroen de Kloet has pointed out, Gang-Tai pop unifies diasporic Chinese with people in Hong Kong, the PRC, and Taiwan to provide "a shared sense of space,"[8] yet the regions' distinctive melodic and visual Mandopop styles also evince strong cultural differences. Similarly, the use of the term "Gang-Tai pop" demonstrates that the PRC is caught between an ideological imperative that Hong Kong and Taiwan are part of China and the recognition that they are distinctive cultural entities.[9]

Since its return to China in 1997, Hong Kong has lost much of its importance in China's imaginary, yet it retains a good deal of political, economic, and cultural distinctiveness, which its movie industry continues to perpetuate. Taiwan's autonomous, if always imperiled, position also acts to legitimate the inner/China vs. outside/Gang-Tai juxtaposition. Because of these political boundaries, Gang-Tai pop also has fairly explicit associations of hybridity with Western musical forms and often gets juxtaposed in PRC discourse with "authentic" Chinese music that is produced in the PRC.

The perception that PRC pop is a poorly made copy of Gang-Tai pop persists in both the PRC[10] and in Taiwan. Since its arrival in the PRC in the late 1970s, Gang-Tai pop has come to represent both what Mandopop is and what it ought to be.[11] Gang-Tai pop's dominance can be found in amateur singing contests on Shanghai's television networks and in the musical choices of department stores and restaurants. When I asked people in Shanghai and Taipei who their favorite performers were, with the exception of mentioning Faye Wong, whose national identity is ambiguous because she is from Beijing but made her career in Hong Kong, not one of the people I interviewed in either Shanghai or Taipei named a PRC performer.

There are many reasons for Gang-Tai pop's success in the PRC. For one, Taiwan and Hong Kong music companies have far more experience in a capitalist supply-and-demand market. Second, the PRC effectively eliminated all but a very few political songs for close to thirty years (1949–1978). Third, both Taiwan and Hong Kong benefited from housing diverse cultural traditions that produced different forms of popular music. In the case of Hong Kong, this took the form of the coexisting, and often symbiotic, music industries of Cantopop (Cantonese pop music) and Mandopop, as well as strong Western musical influences during the British rule from 1897–1997. As I will outline in chapter 3, Taiwan's distinctive music can be credited to its colonial history under Japanese rule (1895–1945), which exposed Taiwanese to the Japanese musical form *enka*, which has had a tremendous influence on Taiyupop (Hokkien dialect pop music, referred to as "Taiwanese language songs," *Taiyu gechu* in Taiwan). In turn, Taiyupop has helped form Mandopop's thematic ethos and melodies, centralizing pervasive themes of melancholy and of women as passive, suffering, and pure. Adding to this mix is a musical cross-dialogue between the Mandopop industries of Taiwan and Hong Kong in conjunction with a continued exposure to music from Japan, Korea, Malaysia, Singapore, and the United States, among others.

The tension between terms such as Gang-Tai pop and Mandopop thereby highlights contested nationalisms that often play themselves out in Mandopop stars' identities. Mandopop diva Faye Wong,[12] for example, moved to Hong Kong in 1987 and, after winning third prize in a singing contest, was signed on with Cinepoly, which immediately transformed her physical image and singing style to blend in better with Hong Kong pop personas. In reinventing her to seem more "cosmopolitan" and "fashionable," her image was localized as a Hong Kong performer.[13] Yet by the time of Hong Kong's repatriation to the PRC in 1997, she had already reasserted her Beijing roots by spending a good deal of time with Beijing rock artists and with statements such as "Beijing is my home: Hong Kong is the office."[14]

Faye Wong's statements seemed quite natural to the people I interviewed in Shanghai, yet one should not overlook that it was precisely the fact that she had established herself outside the PRC's borders that made her so popular.[15] Also, her privileged position in relation to other PRC performers of being able to keep her music production in Hong Kong, where the Chinese government is far less intrusive, keeps her music up to a quality that people enjoy. Faye Wong's career forcefully demonstrates that Mandopop stars' images reaffirm larger conceptions of geographical boundaries while simultaneously demonstrating how easily such boundaries can shift in the public imagination. Further evidence for this can be found in the fact that the people I interviewed in Taiwan disassociated Faye Wong from the PRC by insisting that she is a Hong Kong performer, even when I pointed out that she was originally from Beijing. In contrast, the people I interviewed in Shanghai were unanimous in labeling Faye Wong as a PRC performer because she was originally from Beijing.

Hong Kong performer Sandy Lam and American-born Taiwanese performer David Tao were also linked to Shanghai by people in the PRC who highlighted the performers' Shanghai ancestry. Perhaps the most telling example of the attempt to sinify Gang-Tai pop stars was a woman I interviewed in Shanghai who went so far as to assert that Teresa Teng, Taiwan's most famous performer, had been a spy for the PRC. Though an extreme, this attempt to make Teng more pan-Chinese through an erasure of her Taiwanese identity, aligned with creative narratives about her hidden allegiances, is part of a larger trend in China to adopt Taiwan's performers as their own.

Money Matters and Why Money Matters:
Piracy and a Shifting Music Industry

There are seemingly countless independent Mandopop music labels, but for the most part the Mandopop industry is run by the Taiwan corporation Rock Records and the "Big Five" multinational corporations: EMI (English), Polygram (Dutch); Sony BMG (Japanese and German), Universal (Dutch), and Warner Brothers (American). Rock Records has the highest sales and Mandopop production of these six companies.[16]

By 1966 Taiwan's music industry was already generating US$4.7 million annually.[17] Since that time it has grown exponentially, peaking at just under US$500 million in 1996.[18] The PRC and Taiwan have long been two of the worst copyright infringers in the world,[19] and, as I will outline in chapter 2, the illegal copying of tapes is a significant contributing factor to why Taiwan's Mandopop is so popular in the PRC today.[20] When MP3 downloading became readily accessible, the Mandopop industry began to suffer truly dramatic losses,[21] plummeting from close to US$500 million in 1996[22] to slightly more than US$94 million[23] in 2005.[24]

Because of piracy, breaking the million CD sales mark has always been a challenge for Mandopop stars, but a handful of performers such as A-mei and Jacky Cheung proved that it was possible. Today, even Jay Chou, today's penultimate

Mandopop superstar, is doing well if he can sell 300,000 albums. In 2005 other Mandopop superstars such as Stefanie Sun and Jolin Tsai sold only 100,000 copies of their new albums.[25] CD stores throughout East Asia are closing rapidly and the ones that remain are often a fraction of the size that they once were.

Piracy is hardly surprising given the relatively high cost of CDs in China. While one may find legal Western and Mandopop CDs for as little as US$5, one should keep in mind that the average income in Shanghai is still only US$266 a month[26]—and that is two and a half times China's national average income. Copyright violation also takes on a very different moral valance in the PRC than in the West, for such infringements become the most significant way of subverting state hegemony. In an environment where most mass media is heavily monitored by the state, access to downloaded MP3s, movies, television programs, and news transform what would otherwise be a fairly Orwellian environment into a lifestyle that does not significantly differ from what one might find in other East Asian nations. Most people I have spoken with in Shanghai have seen the latest Hollywood blockbusters, are far more up on American television programming than I am (though admittedly that isn't saying much), and have an impressively international musical repertoire—most of which would not be possible were they to abide by either PRC or Western laws.

In spite of the dramatic losses that downloading has caused, Taiwan's Mandopop industry has been surprisingly resilient—shifting to advertising, concerts, KTV (Taiwan-style karaoke), and movies for its primary revenue. Other innovative money generators include cell phone companies that pay royalties on the tunes its customers choose as their ring tones.[27]

Another result of the changing market is a growing domain for smaller independent record labels. This, in combination with new technology that makes it more affordable to set up one's own recording studio, has resulted in the rise of independent labels that have a much lower overhead than the larger record labels. The grassroots band Sodagreen, for example, sold thirty thousand copies of its album *Little Universe* in 2006, which was more than most of the big record label CDs that year.[28] This propelled the band to become one of most popular Mandopop groups in 2008.

The MP3 phenomenon is also transforming the ways that Mandopop producers are conceptualizing the music industry. George Trivino worked for Rock Records in the late 1990s and currently heads his own independent record label in Taipei with stars such as Chang Cheng Yue and MC Hotdog. This is what he has to say about the ways that MP3s have changed Taiwan's music industry:

In a sense this has resulted in our going back to the very beginning of musical roots. Original music was always live.[. . .] This is the base of music tracing back a thousand years. So in a sense, in playing live music we are getting back to what music should be [. . .]

[After MP3s undermined CD sales] If you make music it is to play it live, it is not just to make a CD. Because if a CD doesn't sell then the artist is gone. But if you are live that is something else. If you look at the U.S. there are a lot of examples of this—like the Grateful Dead and the Rolling Stones—the most classic music and the best music was created by artists whose fan base was created though live performances. In this way, putting out a CD becomes a by-product of the performance, not the other way around.[29]

The growing emphasis on live performances as revenue generators has also been complemented by an increasing degree of grassroots band performances in both China and Taiwan. In Taiwan, singer/songwriter Wu Bai paved the way for this trend as early as the mid-1990s. His popularity in performances caused him to get noticed and signed with a record label rather than the far more common scenario of the record label signing someone and then making him or her a star. The popularity of grassroots performers increased dramatically in 1995 when Western expatriates Mimi Moe and Wade Davis started Spring Scream, an annual beach

Figure I. George Trivino (center), Chang Cheng Yue (right). George Trivino is the manager of Mandopop stars Chang Cheng Yue and MC Hotdog. Photo courtesy of George Trivino.

resort weekend concert for lesser-known bands, which set a trend for a number of other music festivals today.[30] In the PRC, the Beijing rock movement, beginning in the mid-1980s, also set a precedent for grassroots musical styles.

The Shanghai Shift

The dramatic decline in CD sales has created a marked shift in favor of the PRC market. As mentioned above, piracy is also a daunting problem in the PRC, but the population is so large that even if only a small percentage of people buy legal CDs there is still a large market. In the early 1990s, the PRC's total music market was approximately US$143 million[31]—pop music represented 80 percent of that market and Gang-Tai pop accounted for four-fifths of that 80 percent.[32] By 1998 this had doubled and the PRC's legal music market generated US$284 million.[33]

PRC advertising and concerts are increasingly important revenue generators for Taiwan's pop music industry. The most successful Taiwan performers such as Jay Chou, Wang Li-hom, and Jolin Tsai frequently perform in the PRC, and Jonathan Lee, who is arguably the greatest songwriter/composer Taiwan has ever had, has more or less taken up permanent residence there. Rock Records and the Big Five are still based in Taiwan but are increasingly investing in PRC performers.

Shanghai is also becoming the residence of choice for approximately 400,000 Taiwanese businessmen. The reasons for this are many. Taiwan's slowing economy is being dwarfed in the face of the PRC's astounding economic growth. Though more expensive than the rest of China, Shanghai has a lower cost of living, and a potential for lower costs of production, than Taipei. An increasingly tolerant government also makes Shanghai more appealing to live in than at any time since the establishment of the People's Republic of China in 1949. Perhaps most importantly, the large population of Taiwanese in Shanghai, combined with China's current thirst for all things Taiwanese, makes Shanghai a pleasant place to live for Taiwanese expatriates, and one often hears Taipei's businessmen exclaiming that they can live like kings in Shanghai.

The Mandopop industry's shift to the PRC is not without its challenges, however. In addition to the problems of censorship and piracy, there is also the obstacle of operating in China when contracts are not upheld.[34] Since music companies lose money on all but a very few of the most popular artists, for a performer to switch to another company in spite of a contract stipulating further obligation is devastating to the sponsoring company.

In spite of these challenges, the Mandopop industry is clearly not immune to Shanghai's lure, and there is a clear, if gradual, talent drain from Taipei to Shanghai. Yet although it seems likely that Shanghai will be the new center of the Mandopop industry, for the time being it is still a distant third to Taipei and Hong Kong.

KTV Culture—The Embodiment of Song

When I use the term "karaoke" I speak of it as a general term to be found throughout the world. I use the term "KTV" (karaoke TV) to refer to karaoke in Taiwan.[35] Originating in Japan, karaoke arrived in Taiwan in the mid- to late 1970s. As opposed to karaoke's open venues, such as bars, KTV is enclosed in a private room and features microphones and a large television screen which includes the lyrics and features the music videos or, in the case of most Western songs, a low-budget video filmed especially for KTV.[36]

KTV is distinctive from karaoke in several ways. First, in bringing the music to a private room, people sing among friends. This is in direct juxtaposition to karaoke in public venues such as bars in which, as Rob Drew suggests for the United States, karaoke feels liberating precisely because one sings in front of strangers whom one will never see again.[37] In contrast, KTV in the PRC and Taiwan creates a sense of intimacy among the friends sharing the room. As Hiroshi Ogawa notes for Japan, this shared "karaoke space" enforces a sense of belonging within a group while simultaneously allowing them to perform as individuals.[38] The accompanying videos means that in addition to audience members' interaction with each other, there are two visual dramas accompanying the song—the music video and the person or people singing the karaoke song. Through the course of the evening these dramas can overlap or be distinct.

Several scholars have pointed out that karaoke is a technological extension of traditional practices that found a ready market in countries such as England, Japan, Taiwan, and Vietnam, which had long traditions of amateur singing among friends[39] or going out with male friends in the company of hostesses.[40] Yet in addition to being an extension of past tastes and habits, KTV reshapes the present, for it shifts the criterion of many consumers from whether or not one enjoys listening to a song to whether or not it is easy to sing.[41] Because the Mandopop industry is highly sensitive to this point, Mandopop melodies are often relatively simple, avoiding syncopation or erratic stress on particular words and singing softly rather than loudly.

Theo Chou is an American-born Taiwanese who mixes music for popular Taiwanese pop stars such as Fish Leong. He also mixes music for the music producer/songwriter/performer Jonathan Lee (Li Zongshen). Theo Chou notes the important influence that KTV has had on Mandopop melodies.

> Slow songs, like ballad songs, sell the best in Taiwan [. . .] because of the popularity of KTV. Fast songs are hard to sing. People love to sing slow songs and they like the melodies to be simple—because it's easier for them to remember so they can sing along with them. [. . .] For example, right

now I'm working with an artist. She signed with AVEX but she's not out yet. Originally my boss, Jonathan Lee, who's her manager, wanted her music to be more on the heavier side, like more of a rock style with a darker content. But then after doing a rough demo of some of the songs, he took it over to AVEX, the record label, and a lot of the songs got turned down—I wouldn't say they turned them down exactly, but most of their comments were "well, it's not going to sell" or "you need some slow songs." So now I'd say about half of the songs on her album are going to be slow songs.[42]

As another example, Jay Chou, who is known for being one of the least KTV-oriented performers in the industry, stated that five out of twelve songs on his latest release[43] were specifically geared to the KTV market.[44]

KTV has also been a central factor for Gang-Tai pop's success in the PRC in that it serves as advertisements for the songs[45] and exposes Chinese people to a far wider array of Gang-Tai pop than could be seen on state-controlled television programs. As with so many of Taiwan's cultural products in the PRC, Taiwan-style KTV is embedded with symbolic capital in that it is associated with conspicuous consumption and participation in transnational lifestyles. For example, Cashbox, the Taiwanese KTV company, was often lauded by the people I interviewed in Shanghai as being cleaner, more elegant, and, by virtue of being more expensive, a better place to bring someone one wanted to impress.

KTV has been a vital component of the Mandopop industry since the mid-1970s, but since Mandopop sales began to plummet KTV has played a more direct role in generating income for the performers. Claire Hsieh, who plays bass in the Taiwan band Sodagreen, links dwindling CD sales and the emergence of MP3 downloading to the increasing importance of KTV in the Mandopop industry:

> Say we are selling a CD. Now with MP3s a lot of people don't bother buy-ing CDs so we can't make a lot of money in that way. But with KTV they keep track of which songs people choose, and how often, and they give us royalties every time someone selects one of our songs. So the income is a lot more from KTV and it is much more immediate in that KTV organiza-tions pay sooner than the money one gets from CD sales. If a song is popu-lar they will give you NT$200,000 [US$5,882] or NT$300,000 [US$8,824] just for that one song. But if you are selling a CD you only make real money if a lot of people go to buy the CD so the profit margin is smaller.
>
> And often you don't make a lot of money just because a song is popular. There is a sliding scale according to how popular the performer is. So if a performer is very famous KTV gives them a lot more money for

Figure 2. The band Sodagreen benefited greatly from new technologies that allowed for easier access into the music industry for grassroots bands.

> a song. For example, Jay Chou can sell a song for NT$700,000 [US$20,588] but someone else might only get NT$200,000 [US$5,882] for a song—there is a really big difference there. [. . .] And if you have more money then you can produce better quality music so it builds on itself.[46]

In the setting that Claire describes, rather than KTV serving as advertising for CDs, CDs are now marketing for KTV selection. Similarly, a CD's real profit is in building its star's symbolic capital. This allows the stars to obtain better-paying advertisements, parts in movies, and concerts.

KTV as a Gendered Space

If stars perform the concerns of lay people, ordinary people play the role of stars in KTV. Karaoke thereby blurs the boundaries between stars and the average person and between producers and consumers.[47] This gives people the opportunity to try on new identities for size, which can take the form of playing with wildly different roles, as in Casey Lum's study of a reserved father of two college graduates who transformed into a playfully showy young Elvis.[48] Because of the more serious themes of Mandopop, KTV also allows for the opportunity to play an idealized self—revealing a dimension of one's character that is not usually seen.

One of the most fundamental roles that is emphasized in KTV is that of women as performers for male pleasure—a dynamic that dates back to long before the electronic age, when traditional courtesans entertained their guests with song, dance, and lively conversation. With KTV, these roles are perhaps more present in the hostess setting,[49] but even in non-hostess environments, women seem to play a more central role in KTV performance. This is not to say that men do not sing but that women, on the whole, sing more often and put a great deal more effort into preparing for their performances.[50]

As with karaoke in other areas of the world,[51] KTV in the PRC and Taiwan can be used to sing flirtatious lyrics in a way that might be deemed inappropriate in speech. KTV has its own distinctive set of messages, however, for it provides a venue for a range of additional motifs that are more important in Mandopop songs. The centrality of themes of loneliness and heartbreak, for example, allows people to express feelings that are difficult to broach in day-to-day interactions. Because people in the PRC and Taiwan tend to be far less direct than Americans in talking about romance, and because they are far more circumspect in public, parading this different range of emotions becomes a way of avoiding improper displays while also voicing concerns not easily expressed in conversation.

Marilyn Ivy points out that another important dimension of karaoke transcends the auditory experience to allow for a shared "exposure of collective sentimentality" that allows the singer to reveal what he or she is feeling.[52] This is certainly true in KTV as well, for in performing songs of loneliness and heartbreak women emphasize their caring vulnerability[53] and give voice to experiences and feelings that are difficult to share in normal conversation. As an extension of the prevalent themes of loneliness and heartbreak in Mandopop, it is quite common for women to break into tears while singing at KTV.[54]

Singing also allows women and men to play out gendered identities, creating a habitus that naturalizes such roles through daily actions.[55] A KTV performance carries an implicit understanding that choosing a song not only reflects the aesthetic tastes of the KTV singer but often becomes a public statement to friends and lovers about their innermost feelings through singing other's lyrics. As an extension of this, in the PRC, KTV has provided a venue to express previously proscribed sentiments in a language provided by Gang-Tai pop from beyond its borders.

Chapter Overviews

Chapters 2 and 3 provide the historical background necessary to understand the contemporary Mandopop scene. In chapter 2 I examine China's musical history, beginning with the birth of Chinese popular music in the East Asian jazz mecca of 1920s Shanghai and tracing musical and cultural developments to the present day. This will include a brief overview of alternative musical genres in the PRC such as Beijing rock and revolutionary opera, among others. The chapter concludes with an examination of the important manner in which Taiwan's musical ethos has influenced the PRC music industry and the ways in which Taiwan's Mandopop has served as a middle zone by introducing Western music and cultural values to the PRC. The chapter concludes by exploring Taiwan pop's role in exporting a very different version of womanhood to the PRC—directly confronting and subverting PRC state attempts at gender erasure from 1949 through the 1970s as well as contemporary masculinist discourse.

Chapter 3 presents Taiwan's musical history and explores the issue of why Taiwan pop is so appealing to Chinese-speaking audiences throughout the world. In this chapter I focus on the music's exceptional hybridity, beginning with foreign influences during Taiwan's colonial history under the Dutch and the Japanese, and continuing with Taiwan's political, cultural, and economic alliance with the United States and the resulting wealth of transnational musical influences from the rest of East Asia and the United States. I then address the appeal of this musical mixing for Mandopop audiences in both the PRC and Taiwan.

In chapter 4 I explore the surprisingly ubiquitous themes of loneliness and isolation in Taiwan's Mandopop songs. This, more than any other facet of the music, has separated it from the PRC's musical genres, which have traditionally demanded a fanatically cheerful thematic intensity to celebrate the state. The range of emotional expression evinced in Taiwan's songs of sorrow resonates strongly in the PRC.

In chapter 5 I explore the ways in which women's identities are constructed in Mandopop. For one, most female performers sing songs that are written by men. Of course, this can also be said of many U.S. pop songs. The difference is that in China and Taiwan songwriters are famous in their own right and therefore the audience's categorization of a song as a "woman's song," in spite of common knowledge that a man wrote the song, highlights the fact that women are active participants in male lyricists' depictions of seemingly innate differences between women and men.

Chapter 6 explores masculine identities in Mandopop. Mandopop's *wenrou* male—which translates into English as tender, sensitive, and somewhat androgynous by Western standards—directly counters the hypermasculine ethos of PRC-produced revolutionary songs or Beijing rock. Male performer's identities are remarkably flexible compared to their female counterparts, and the typical male artist will shift from *wenrou* to bad boy with chameleon-like ease.

The book concludes with an unavoidably polemic view of the widespread condemnation of Mandopop. One hears a wide range of critiques of Mandopop in both Chinese and English-language scholarship, popular press, and casual conversations. Drawing on both the data and analysis from the earlier chapters, chapter 7 asks the simple question: If the music is as bad as these critics assert, why is it so central to the lives of the largest population in the world? I will argue that the critiques of Mandopop tell us more about the reviewers' personal and cultural biases than the music itself, and I will highlight Mandopop's important contribution as a modern-day poetic lament that simultaneously embraces and protests modern life.

Conclusion

I would like to conclude this introduction by asking some preliminary questions that will be addressed in the following chapters concerning the cultural implications of Mandopop. Does Mandopop symbolize the transnational or the local? Is it an example of men's creation of women's mass-mediated roles or is it a reflection of women's perceptions of themselves? Is the apolitical nature of Mandopop an intensely political stance given the totalitarian histories of Chinese-speaking nations? Do songs of despair reflect growing discontent among modern urban youth, or, in venting grief through listening to and singing such songs, do people gain the catharsis that allows them to lead otherwise healthy lives? If men seem to feel more comfortable listening to women singing songs of loneliness that express anomie, feelings of dependence, passivity, and despair, is it because they see women as naturally aligned with these roles or is it because men also want to express these emotions but are culturally discouraged from doing so? As will become clear in the following chapters, in spite of the seemingly contradictory nature of these queries, one must in fact answer in the affirmative to each component of these questions. This attests to the cultural complexity of these songs and why they are so important if we hope to come to a better understanding of China and Taiwan.

CHAPTER 2

China's Mandopop Roots and Taiwan's Gendered Counter-Invasion of the PRC

Chinese popular music is less a mere adjunct to leisure than a battle-field on which ideological struggle is waged.
—Andrew Jones, *Like a Knife: Ideology and Genre in Contemporary Chinese Popular Music*

Noisy? Your jazz is quieter, then? I had to listen to a little of it the other day, and it's nothing more than a gang of shrine noise-makers in foreign clothes. If that's what you want, you can find any amount in Japan without bothering to import it.
—Junichirō Tanizaki, *Some Prefer Nettles*

This chapter will trace China's musical history, beginning with Shanghai's jazz era in the first half of the twentieth century to contemporary PRC music. I will also examine the effects of Gang-Tai pop (Hong Kong and Taiwan pop) on the PRC's musical and cultural ethos, concluding with an exploration of the gendered identities that this music has exported to the PRC.

Shanghai's Jazz Era, 1911–1937

Western music accompanied Christian missionaries' arrival in China beginning in 1601, when Matteo Ricci brought a harpsichord to China and trained eunuchs to perform Chinese songs to please the imperial court.[1] This expanded in the early 1800s, when American Protestant missionaries began bringing hymn books to China,[2] and then with the May Fourth Movement of 1919, which spurred an effort to modernize by emulating the West, including training Chinese musicians in Western musical education.[3]

In 1842 Western powers, including France, Germany, and England, established foreign districts in Shanghai as part of a series of treaties. China was so far behind militarily that it had no choice but to acquiesce. While this created a good deal of resentment, the power of the West was seductive to many Chinese, and a myriad of cultural products ranging from fashion to cinema to music became the hottest trends in urban centers across the country.

As is the case today, Shanghai was at the forefront of China's modernization. From 1848 to 1908 Shanghai sported the latest modern technology—ranging from electricity and running water to open boulevards that allowed for trams and automobiles. Indeed, at that time, Shanghai could be said to rival any city in the world for modern conveniences.[4] Jazz, the ultimate symbol of modern urban sophistication in the early twentieth century, found a welcome home in Shanghai, and jazz artists from as far as Japan would sojourn there to hone their skills.[5]

Because of Japan's military aggression and China's ongoing civil war, the first half of the twentieth century was an uncertain time in China. Yet far from discouraging early club culture, the political turmoil only seemed to fan the flame of living for the moment.[6] Shanghai natives flocked to the first dance halls in droves as soon as they were opened in the early 1920s,[7] and the curfews set up during the 1920s civil war only resulted in clubgoers being locked in cabarets and nightclubs until dawn.[8] By the mid-1930s there were more than three hundred cabarets in Shanghai alone.[9]

In the 1930s, Shanghai's population reached almost 3.5 million—making it the fourth largest city in the world at the time. As in contemporary Shanghai, much of the population was made up of Chinese people from other areas who were drawn to Shanghai because of its employment possibilities. The foreign feel of Shanghai related to the Western imperialist presence, but it also owed a good deal to Russians fleeing a civil war in 1922 who opened beauty parlors and small shops and who engaged in prostitution or performed in cabarets.[10] From 1933 to 1941 Shanghai also housed approximately 200,000 Jewish refugees from Germany. Shanghai's jazz movement followed music and dance trends from the West such as the cha-cha, fox-trot, rumba, waltz, and tango introduced by East Indian, Filipino, Indonesian, and Russian bands, who played both their own music and local pop for the Euro-American expatriate community and for the Chinese elite.[11]

Western cinema arrived in Shanghai in 1896 and quickly became the center of the Chinese film industry. By 1927 there were 106 movie theaters in China with a total of approximately sixty-eight thousand seats—26 of these theaters were in Shanghai.[12] By the 1930s it was common to hand out sheet music to movie audiences, and the music often outlasted the movies in popularity.[13] Cinema would continue to be an essential venue for promoting pop music from that moment onward.[14]

Another technological innovation that would transform the nature of Chinese popular music was the gramophone, which limited songs to 2.5 to 3.5 minutes to fit on the records. This served to standardize regional differences, bring music from clubs to the home, and offer access to Western musical trends such as jazz to a much wider audience.[15] In 1923, before it was affordable for people to own their own gramophones, wealthy Chinese in Shanghai would pay people to bring gramophones to their houses for special events.[16] Gramophones thereby became an emblem of modernity and a marker of class as there was a shift in focus from public gatherings to private consumption.[17]

In much of East Asia, the 1920s saw the beginning of mass-produced pop as large music companies, funded by foreign capital, spread their roots.[18] The raw volume of record production by transnational companies was astounding—2.7 million records a year were produced in China in the early twentieth century,[19] and there were 1.1 million imported records to China from the United States and Europe in 1929 alone.[20] In 1932, China's domestic production and consumption of records had grown to 5.4 million albums a year, with thousands of records being exported to other nations such as Indonesia.[21]

By the 1930s, Shanghai's publishing houses were producing so many novels, magazines, newspapers, and tabloids that in one year they would publish the same volume that the entire U.S. publication industry had produced in its lifetime.[22] Shanghai's musical renaissance drew on this powerful literary explosion and many of the lyricists were either journalists or novelists.[23]

Most Chinese intellectuals fled Shanghai during the Japanese occupation (November 12, 1937, to August 15, 1945), and for the most part they headed south to regions such as Hong Kong.[24] Worried that mass media would stir unrest, the Japanese army closed down theaters, newspapers, and publishing houses, effectively ending Shanghai's musical renaissance. When China's KMT (Kuomintang) government regained control of Shanghai in 1945 things did not improve. By this time the KMT had whipped itself into an anticommunist frenzy, and it continued policies of repression by imposing censorship, putting spies in schools and university campuses, and massacring young communists.[25] When it became clear that the communists would be victorious in their revolution, a second wave of migration effectively transferred the hub of Chinese popular music to Hong Kong for the next twenty years.

1949 to 1978

The Chinese Communist Party had been employing music as a means of propaganda since the 1930s.[26] Mao Zedong's 1942 "Talks at the Yan'an Conference on Literature and Art" explicitly stated that art had an obligation to serve the people, which effectively silenced alternative political and musical voices.[27] Beginning with the establishment of the People's Republic of China in 1949, "revolutionary songs" (geming gequ) and "revolutionary operas" (geming geju), designed to whip the populace into a patriotic fervor, became the sole acceptable means of musical expression. By the Cultural Revolution (1966–1976) there were only eight operas and ballets permitted to be performed in all of China.[28]

The "East Is Red" is without question the most emblematic revolutionary song of this era:

THE EAST IS RED (Dongfang hong)

Dongfang hong.	The East is red.
Taiyang shang.	The sun is rising.
Zhongguo chule ge Mao Zedong.	China has brought forth Mao Zedong.
Ta wei renmin mo xinfu.	He has a plan to bring the Chinese people good fortune.
Huerhaiya, ta shi renmin da jiuxing.	Hooray,[29] he is the people's great savior.

"The East Is Red" is credited to Li Louyuan, a poor farmer who applied his own lyrics to a popular folk melody. When Tian Han, the man who wrote the national anthem, was imprisoned during the Cultural Revolution, "The East Is Red" became the de facto national song. Revolutionary songs and operas were banned after the Cultural Revolution[30] but would make a comeback in the mid-1980s, when it became popular to combine Maoist revolutionary songs with a disco beat.

In the 1970s, Western music and Gang-Tai pop began to be smuggled into the PRC through Taiwan and Hong Kong.[31] This was assisted by Taiwan's government, which routinely floated balloons with canned food and tapes of Teresa Teng's music across the Taiwan Strait.[32] For many people in the PRC, Gang-Tai pop produced some of the earliest samples of contemporary life coming from the outside world.[33] Taiwan came to act as a middle zone that exposed the PRC to Western and alternative Asian forms of modernity that represented more active participation in global culture.[34]

My Shanghai interviews overwhelmingly cited Taiwanese performer Teresa Teng (Deng Lijun) as the leader of this change. Alice, a twenty-five-year-old college graduate in Shanghai, provides a representative statement to this effect here:

[The Gang-Tai invasion] began with Teresa Teng and then with people like Fei Xiang, an American-born Chinese singer who also came to China in the 1980s. Before Teresa Teng no one listened to pop music. It was all revolutionary songs. It was Teng that ushered in love songs. Her stuff was really great because she sang about real life issues, not just about politics. [. . .] My mom loves Teresa Teng and all the other music from that era. My folks were in their twenties and thirties at that time, and that is the age when people usually listen to pop music, right?

Teresa Teng's stuff is remade by a lot of people today, like Faye Wong and many others. If you had to choose one star and say "she is the absolute most important pop singer in the history of Chinese pop music" there is no doubt it would be Teresa Teng.[35]

As Nimrod Baranovitch has stated, Teresa Teng's musical arrival in the PRC was "like a dry field in which a match had been thrown."[36] Even before it was legal to buy her music in the PRC, contraband tapes made her popular enough that it was said that "Old Deng [Xiaoping] rules by day, Little Deng [Lijun] rules by night."[37] Her musical presence was the beginning of a new era of PRC emulation of Taiwan's fashion and songs. Performers throughout the PRC vied to hold the title as their particular club's "Little Deng Lijun"[38] in much the same way that PRC performer Hu Yanbin is referred to as "Little Jay"[39] today. Andrew Jones notes that the PRC songwriters he interviewed in the late 1980s uniformly spoke of being exposed to Teresa Teng's songs in 1978 and 1979 as the deciding factor in their decision to pursue careers in the pop music industry and that they took Gang-Tai pop as the model for what Mandopop should be.[40]

1978 to 1989

Almost immediately after Mao Zedong's death in 1976 the Gang of Four was arrested and Deng Xiaoping paved the way for capitalism with his Open Door Policy of 1978 and his 1979 call for "socialism with Chinese characteristics." As Timothy Brace has pointed out, the initial flood of Gang-Tai music was done "half openly" in that people could legally buy or copy cassettes brought in from the outside, but it was still not broadcasted on state-controlled television or radio.[41] This was closely connected with new technologies such as cassette tapes and tape recorders that were affordable for the first time, freeing many people from being bound to state-endorsed media such as public concerts, radio, or television shows.[42]

The shock and excitement of being exposed to Gang-Tai pop after a twenty-year state monopoly on music cannot be overemphasized. During the Cultural Revolution, personal emotions were to be subsumed to devotion to the state or to Mao (which amounted to the same thing). Teresa Teng's songs, and other Mandopop from beyond PRC's borders, expressed human emotions that had been purged from China's musical repertoire in the previous decades.[43]

As Miss Li, a twenty-eight-year-old nurse in Shanghai, notes:

One problem with Chinese music as opposed to Gang-Tai pop is that our government felt that love was a distraction for youth—that they should focus their hearts and minds on the nation. In a way this wasn't such a new concept—before that, Chinese people always told their children to focus on their studies and they discouraged courtship because the parents thought it would distract their children from achieving greatness in their studies and careers. So, when Taiwanese love songs, like those by Teresa Teng, came to China it was not only good music, it was a whole new concept—a foreign idea really, that love and individual desire were ok.[44]

As Alice and Miss Li emphasize, Teresa Teng's focus on romance, rather than on the state, represented a dramatic shift in perspective. Gang-Tai pop lyrics provided a space for listeners to develop a new vocabulary for the expression of individuality or the self (*ziwo, zijue*)[45] and a sense of women's consciousness (*nüxing yishi*).[46] As an extension of this, Gang-Tai pop songs included lyrics in which women lamented losing their sense of self (*meiyou ziji, wuwo*) in unhealthy relationships.[47] Far from being glorified as a prerequisite to becoming a loyal citizen of the state, this selflessness was now cast in the new dimension of a romantic tragedy.

As the PRC's government began to withdraw financial support for the arts as part of a larger move toward a capitalist free market, China's music industries had to learn how to survive through sales rather than relying on state subsidies.[48] This resulted in more traditional musical forms, such as Peking opera, being all but eradicated in open-market competition with Mandopop.[49]

Gang-Tai pop culture was more accessible to people in the PRC than was Western culture because of shared linguistic, aesthetic, and cultural traditions. The PRC government continued to ban most European and American music and music videos on the grounds that they were too violent, sexually suggestive, and individualistic, which effectively gave Gang-Tai pop an open market with little competition from the West. Because of its heavy Western influences, Gang-Tai pop effectively served as a translation point between East and West, which, however, resulted in the PRC state's condemnation of the music. Today, the PRC's government has been forced to allow Gang-Tai pop as the overwhelming mandate of the people, but this opening of China's borders was not without a struggle.

Gang-Tai pop songs and visual imagery from the 1970s and 1980s were remarkably restrained in comparison with pre-1949 Shanghai era, contemporary Mandopop, or Western popular music.[50] Yet compared to what PRC audiences and government officials had seen in the previous thirty years, Gang-Tai pop's lyrical and visual presentations were nothing less than revolutionary. The PRC government had an extremely hostile reaction to Gang-Tai pop during this period, going so far as to label the music "obscene," "pornographic," "spiritual pollution," "imperialist and bourgeois ideology," "morally decadent and aesthetically empty." The music was castigated as an emasculated "illness that was inherited from the

1930s" and labeled as "the sounds of a subjugated nation."[51] In the early 1980s, people in the PRC could be arrested simply for listening to Gang-Tai pop that was not approved by the state.[52]

In the mid-1980s the question shifted from how to censor pop music to how to co-opt it for the state's own uses.[53] Television sets and radios aided in the promotion of popular music, though this was of course under far more control than cassettes.[54] The first airing of Gang-Tai pop as music videos was in 1984.[55] Gang-Tai campus folk songs such as "My Chinese Heart" (Wo de Zhongguo xin)[56] were fabulously popular in the PRC,[57] but the songs' patriotic themes forcefully demonstrated the government's continued presence in monitoring mass media.

In 1986 the PRC began releasing its own pop with the overt intention of "opposing" (fankang) Gang-Tai pop. PRC pop songs were supposed to be more grounded in local culture (bentuhua) and to better reflect the Chinese race (minzuhua).[58] The music industry thereby became a political and cultural battle zone between Gang-Tai's perceived "Western" individualistic themes of love and the PRC focus on Chinese national identity and culture.

New Technologies—PRC Pop and its Limitations

In the 1980s, television programming featuring Mandopop singing competitions reached an estimated 700 million people, which represented 68 percent of the Chinese population.[59] By the mid-1990s an estimated 900 million people were watching television in China and more than 90 percent of urban households had televisions.[60]

In 1991 the first PRC-produced music videos were aired in China,[61] with the predictable emphasis on indigenization (minzuhua).[62] The first Chinese music programming was aired on China's new Music Television (MTV) in 1993 and consisted of Taiwanese programming for the most part.[63] In fact, Gang-Tai pop was such a large presence that it has been suggested that "if there were no Gang-Tai pop, there would be no MTV."[64]

The PRC government quickly reacted against these outside influences. The head of CCTV, whose official title was vice minister of China's Radio, Film, and Television Ministry, emphasized that "music television has to carry on and develop China's traditional culture, and reflect the deep love of the people toward the homeland and life."[65] In 1993, four hundred MTV videos were produced for China's MTV including Gang-Tai songs such as "I am Chinese" (Wo shi Zhongguoren).[66] The goal, it was stated, was a purposeful sinification (Zhongguohua) of Mandopop in order to "reflect China's 5,000 year cultural history."[67] China's MTV videos often created nationalist images such as a view of China's national flag or pictures of the Great Wall that supported the song's political lyrics—or they were simply inserted into the visuals even though they had nothing to do with a particular song's lyrics.[68] In the same year, as part of a "fight against the evil influences" of Gang-Tai pop, China held a televised music competition for one hundred Chinese pop songs that were to be "suitable to traditional morality, to sing of a beautiful life, and to reflect society's development."[69] The songs were to demonstrate a sense of the Chinese race (*minzuhua*) and "Chinese characteristics" (*Zhongguo tese*).[70] Later, "rules of conduct" such as "love the motherland, the people and the Communist Party of China. Do homework conscientiously. Keep clothes tidy and clean. Do not spit" became central themes of PRC pop,[71] as did a musical call for good citizenship and productivity.[72]

As opposed to the pervasive melancholy of Gang-Tai pop, PRC pop's seemingly relentless optimism celebrated China's greatness with songs such as "The Great Wall of China Is Long" (Changcheng chang) or the "Valiant Spirit of Asia." Nimrod Baranovitch notes that songs lauding Beijing, the center of the PRC's government, were common, whereas songs praising Shanghai, Guangzhou, or other urban centers of China were conspicuously absent.[73] These political songs included a call for "good citizenship, collectivism, productivity, education, the centrality of Beijing, Chinese sovereignty [. . .] over Hong Kong (before 1997) and Tibet.[74]

In 1996 the PRC held a televised singing competition in which performers were required to demonstrate a "warm love for the homeland, and observe discipline and abide by the law."[75] In 2001 it held another music competition titled "China's indigenous (*bentu*) pop songs MTV competition."[76] Not unlike America's moral crusades against hip-hop lyrics, the PRC's repeated attempts to monitor the morality of pop (and in the case of the PRC to assert nationalist values) merely served to advertise the music that it protested. Since 1990 the most popular commercial PRC pop singers, such as Yang Yuying, have been more closely aligned with Gang-Tai visual and melodic representation than with state-endorsed attempts to make pop.[77]

As a reflection of the government's growing awareness that its citizens have less tolerance for overt political lecturing than it once had, the state-run MTV programs rotate a mixture of highly politicized songs with other songs whose propaganda value is less overt, to some songs with no political message at all—essentially sugar-coating its propaganda tool to gain more effectiveness.[78] Indeed, in recent years, the PRC state's power to control mass media has been quickly eroding as people have gained more access to satellite TV, travel, and pirated goods from abroad. Today most of the televised amateur singing contests feature contestants who, for the most part, choose to perform Gang-Tai pop. CD sales, KTV selections, and daily conversations all reflect the fact that Taiwan pop, especially, is the voice of China's modern age.

There was an almost unanimous sentiment among the people I interviewed in both Shanghai and Taipei that the quality of PRC pop is still thematically and melodically far behind Gang-Tai pop,[79] though several people in Shanghai argued that it is catching up fast. As noted above, there are several reasons why PRC pop still lags behind Gang-Tai pop in spite of the PRC's huge population and its ample resources. The most important of these is the PRC government's repeated attempts to shift the focus from what people want to hear to what it feels they *should* want to hear, evincing a parental frustration and lack of understanding concerning why its subjects/children/citizens do not choose what is best for them. Yet, although the state maintains control of mass-mediated production, one must also recognize the limits of state hegemony, its responsiveness to audience/citizen's demands, and its remarkable adaptability to a new technological world that has exposed its citizens to thoughts and modes of behavior that they did not have access to in the past. In a very Foucaultian sense, is a mistake to think of the state as a unified force, for the government is made up of many different factions[80] that might be as diverse as there are individuals in government offices, some of whom may be fans. This might explain why the government asked PRC rock star Cui Jian to perform to raise money for the Asian games and then withdrew the invitation, and why it criticized Hong Kong performer Anita Mui's music as being lascivious and pornographic while some government officials curried favor with her.[81]

In a moment, I will compare the gendered imagery surrounding Taiwan's Mandopop and PRC music. Before I can do so, however, a brief overview of these musical forms seems in order.

Beijing Rock

The Beijing rock movement appeared in China in the mid-1980s and by 1990 it was an established subculture in Beijing. In contrast with the Mandopop industry, the rock movement in both the PRC and Taiwan was a grassroots movement in that bands first gathered a local fan base and then got signed on with record companies.[82] Although rock artists conceptualize the genre as being opposed to pop, Beijing rock can also said to be born out of pop roots, as opposed to contemporary pop's birth from rock in the West. Today, its identity very much continues to be shaped in opposition to Gang-Tai pop.[83]

The PRC government's repression of Beijing rock is hardly surprising given rock's antiestablishment rebellion against the state.[84] Ironically, it is the state's presence that fosters an environment for rock; in "free" societies such as Hong Kong and Taiwan, where there is less to fight against, there is little interest in this musical genre.

Beijing rock was at its height during the Tiananmen protests of 1989. Although Beijing rock artists are increasingly trying to disassociate themselves from politics, their lyrics continue to be highly nationalistic, and rock performers contrast their own music as authentically Chinese with Gang-Tai pop as Western or foreign.[85] This overlooks the obvious Western origins of rock as well as the continued practice of employing images that directly align Beijing rock with its Western counterparts.[86] The claim that Beijing rock is "purely Chinese" is also clearly antiquated in today's global economy in that Beijing rock relies on funding from the Gang-Tai pop music industry, which "imports" the music back into China.[87]

Beijing rock continues to hold the attention of many Chinese and Taiwanese musicians, as well as Western academics, but it has never represented more than a small fraction of the Chinese-language music market. By 1994 Beijing rock was already in decline in favor of Gang-Tai pop, even in Beijing where rock had traditionally had its strongest audience.[88] One reason for this is that Beijing rock is commonly dismissed as elitist because its fan base is almost exclusively made up of Beijing's elite, including artists, intellectuals, students, and the independently wealthy.[89] PRC scholar Huang Hao has emphasized this point by quoting a man he interviewed, who asked, "who has time to indulge in drink, sex and drugs?"[90]

Another part of the move away from Beijing rock was a post-Tiananmen cynicism about one's ability to change anything.[91] China's almost rabid embrace of capitalism has also made Beijing rock's relatively political messages seem dated—a residual effect of the political idealism that directly preceded the Tiananmen era, as well as the hyperpolitical times of the first three decades of communist rule. In today's China, people are willingly self-censoring in exchange for economic prosperity and relative freedom in other aspects,[92] and as the memory of the Tiananmen demonstrations fades, Beijing rock's potency flounders in a sea of political apathy.

Tongsu Music

Tongsu music (*tongsu yinyue*) means "music for the masses." It is distinctive from Mandopop in that *tongsu* focuses on socialist ideals and praise of the state, but it has never posed a real threat to either the PRC's Mandopop industry or to Gang-Tai pop. As Huang Hao quips, the 1970s featured governmentally sponsored *tongsu* music as part of a larger policy to serve the people (*wei renmin fuwu*), whereas the 1980s saw the dominance of Gang-Tai pop in which the free market shifted the focus to "serve the people's money" (*wei renminbi fuwu*).[93]

Xibeifeng

The *xibeifeng* (the northwest wind) musical movement of the mid-1980s was heavily tied to the film industry, getting its start in movies such as Zhang Yimou's *Red Sorghum*.[94] Like *tongsu* music, it was introduced by the state-controlled music industry as a direct attempt to wrest cultural hegemony from the hands of Taiwan and Hong Kong.[95] Fusing folk music with disco beats and lyrically focusing on problems of modern society, as Mercedes Dujunco states, "in *xibeifeng*, we find the Chinese legendary past linked with the globalized modern present."[96] In turn, the *xibeifeng* movement is commonly dismissed as state propaganda. As Li Luxin quips, although the "northwest wind" was meant to compete with Gang-Tai pop, "the real wind was coming from Taiwan and Hong Kong," and the PRC could hardly hope to compete.[97]

Revolutionary Disco

In the mid-1980s, revolutionary songs, including "The East Is Red," were reissued with a new disco beat. This is simultaneously seen as the government's attempt to restore patriotic fervor[98] as well as a direct critique of economic reforms, which, while providing welcome opportunities, also left many unemployed and unprotected.[99] Thus, this musical genre is rich in contradictions in that it paradoxically both celebrates and subverts the state through its camp.

When Yin Defeats Yang: Exporting Taiwan's Gender Identities to the PRC

Taiwan pop's tremendous influence on the PRC has been accompanied by a range of new gender identities that stand in contrast with the hypermasculine ethos of musical trends in the PRC. Though Beijing rock was a grassroots movement rising out of intellectual circles and *xibeifeng* was state-endorsed, both share several common characteristics: both the *xibeifeng* and Beijing rock movements began in the mid-1980s as a direct attempt to wrest cultural hegemony from the hands of Taiwan and Hong Kong. Each of these musical genres claimed to be more authentically Chinese than Gang-Tai pop, and each is notable for its nationalistic and masculinist imagery conveyed with loud booming melodies which stand in marked contrast to the soft, wispy, apolitical voices of Gang-Tai pop.[100]

The masculine rock/feminine pop dichotomy is analogous to conceptions of the rock/pop divide in the West. What makes the Chinese case distinctive is its alignment along geographical terrains of the political North (Beijing) and the commercialized South (Hong Kong and Taiwan).[101] This geographical divide has a second dimension in that the northern sphere houses the PRC government whereas Hong Kong and Taiwan still retain political autonomy in the south. This, in turn, overlaps with the commonly found conceptual split between the PRC as "authentically Chinese" vs. Gang-Tai's "foreign influences."

Beijing rock artists' claims that rock's masculinized identity is somehow more authentically Chinese conveniently overlooks rock's Western origins, and their masculinist-nationalist rhetoric concerning the pernicious cultural influences of popular culture from Taiwan and Hong Kong sounds remarkably like the state's stance. In both the PRC state and Beijing rock discourse, the hypermasculine Beijing comes to represent "authentic" Chineseness while southern metropolises such as Hong Kong, Shanghai, and Taipei signify a feminine and Westernized other.

Yet none of the masculinized forms of music—ranging from revolutionary disco to Beijing rock to *xibeifeng*—have provided serious competition for Gang-Tai pop. In fact, even the people I interviewed in Shanghai were hard-pressed to name a PRC rock or *xibeifeng* song that they liked, and although many of the people I interviewed in Taipei had heard of some of the more popular rock performers such as Cui Jian, most of them could not even name a PRC-produced song.

The self-defined masculinist identity of the PRC music industries, in contrast to the feminized image of Gang-Tai pop, is generally accepted by people in the PRC but is often employed in very different ways than the state intended. For example, Amanda, a twenty-three-year-old college graduate looking for work in Shanghai, portrayed Beijing masculinist culture as being somewhat uncouth in relation to feminine Shanghai and Taiwan culture:

> Shanghai, Hong Kong, and Taiwan are very close in lifestyles and attitudes. Beijing is very different—sort of backwards compared to Shanghai, Taiwan, and Hong Kong, which are more international and modern. You can tell if someone is not from Shanghai just by looking at them. For instance, that guy over there [She discreetly points to a man sitting across the room], he's not from Shanghai. Look at his hairdo and his clothes— and his mannerisms! Shanghai people are more sophisticated I think. [...] Guys in Beijing are too macho, they like to work out all the time and have big muscles. Shanghai guys are not so strong but they are better looking.[102]

Amanda supports conceptual boundaries of the masculine northern state culture vs. southern feminized commercial one. Importantly, however, she inverts the state hierarchy associated with this dichotomy by placing Beijing's masculinized culture at the bottom and preferring instead to link Shanghai's culture with Taiwan and Hong Kong as both proudly feminine and cosmopolitan. Amanda is not alone in her views. Most of the people I interviewed in Shanghai aligned Beijing's macho culture with undesirable state politics in contrast to modern global sophistication that southern and feminized Taiwan, Hong Kong, or Shanghai represent.[103]

This creates an interesting tension, for while the PRC and its music industries proclaim their music to be China's masculine and authenticated self, the vast majority of people I have spoken with in both Shanghai and Taipei prefer the lyrical themes and the visual presentation of the "feminine" other in Gang-Tai pop.

Mr. Chen, a thirty-year-old employee at a cell phone company in Shanghai, essentially suggests that Taiwan's songs have more soul, for example:

> I like women's songs better than men's songs. [. . .] Women's songs really make you feel something whereas men's songs tend to be a bit more superficial. Taiwan makes really good women's songs—they are more moving than songs from Hong Kong or China.[104]

Miss Wang, an elementary school teacher from Shenzhen who had come to Shanghai to be with her fiancé, also favorably commented on the more "feminine" culture of Taiwan.

> I like Taiwanese women's accents—women sound very tender (*wenrou*)—I also think Taiwan's musicians are popular because they have better clothing and makeup.[105]

Christian, a thirty-year-old female who works at an advertising company in Shanghai, reflects prevailing conceptions of gendered urban identities:

> I think in the north of China rock and roll are more popular than here in Shanghai. You know, it goes with their personalities because they are a lot more macho—they have bigger muscles and they are more sexist (*zhong nan qing nü*). That's why Gang-Tai pop is so popular, because it is very southern and the men are much more feminine—that goes better with the pop image. Shanghai is in between I think. Shanghai men are famous for cooking and shopping but they don't talk or act as feminine as Taiwan guys.[106]

The concept of "authentic" Chineseness is a top-down state or elite rock call for masculine nationalist strength, yet the vast majority of urban Chinese are voting for Gang-Tai pop culture with both their wallets and their hearts. What is authentically Chinese thereby proves to be precisely Gang-Tai pop's feminine-coded musical hybridity with the West that rock, *xibeifeng*, and the PRC state condemn.[107]

Conclusion

In contemporary mass-mediated culture, the sensitive (*wenrou*) male stands for antitraditionalism in portraying vulnerable non-patriarchal men.[108] Beijing rock artists and fans see their music as an effort to recover a masculinity (expressed through anger, rabid individualism, and loud music) that they feel has been lost under state control and traditional Confucian values that suppress individual desire.[109] Huang Hao notes that the Beijing rock group Tang Dynasty's band members, for example, overtly identify themselves with ancient martial artists who combine "poetic refinement of the literati and the technical prowess of legendary swordsmen."[110] In turn, *xibeifeng* evokes images of "ethnic minority virility" with its "rough vocal delivery."[111] In contrast, Mandopop celebrates an image of fragile men that is arguably closer to traditional elite Chinese ideals of manhood.[112]

Although Gang-Tai pop themes are arguably conservative in their presentation of gender relations, they also present the feminine as more noble in her suffering, more desirable in her appearance and behavior, and more modern in her globalized, rather than national, images. The fact that both women and men seem to identify with this feminized musical sphere and its embodied identities is nothing short of a gendered revolution.

CHAPTER 3

Hybridity and Its Discontents

Popular Music in Taiwan

Who is to say that Mickey Mouse is not Japanese, or that Ronald
McDonald is not Chinese? To millions of children who watch Chinese
television, "Uncle McDonald" (alias Ronald) is probably more familiar
than the mythical characters of Chinese folklore.

—James Watson, *Golden Arches East: McDonald's in East Asia*

These ancient painters never succeeded in denationalizing themselves.
The Italian artists painted Italian Virgins, the Dutch painted Dutch
Virgins, the Virgins of the French painters were Frenchwomen. [. . .]
Can it be possible that the painters make John the Baptist a Spaniard
in Madrid and an Irishman in Dublin?

—Mark Twain, *The Innocents Abroad*

On September 9, 2003, I was in Taipei, Taiwan, at Eslite,[1] an upscale
twenty-four-hour coffee shop and bookstore, taking a break from the tri-
als and tribulations of fieldwork. As a diversion, I purchased the Chinese
translation of *Memoirs of a Geisha*[2]—a fictional autobiography of a Japanese geisha
written by a Caucasian male from the United States. On the way home, I walked
along Zhong Xiao East Road, one of the most fashionable shopping districts in
Taiwan, and then through some back alleys behind the Japanese department store
Sogo. My fellow pedestrians included affluent Chinese youth flaunting the latest
fashions, an old gnarled man in a pointed straw hat hobbling through the crowd,
the occasional Japanese or American businessman, and a few Filipina women ani-
matedly speaking Tagalog as they waited for their friend who was talking on a
payphone. Singaporean Stefanie Sun's music was gently playing in the background
at the 7-11 where I stopped off to choose between my customary Marlboros or the
Taiwanese brand "Long Life Cigarettes" (Changshou yan).

During my return journey, Taiwanese performer Jay Chou's most recent hit
blared from a clothing store specializing in pirated Western designer clothes, which

added to the lively atmosphere[3] of the street vendors selling steak and noodles, stinky tofu, and shaved ice on food stands in the street in front of the store. This is downtown Taipei—an urban mix of some of the most elite transnational hybridity in the world, with traditional Taiwanese sights and odors oozing through every crack in the pavement.

This intensely hybrid environment is in large part the reason for Taiwan's exceptionally rich cultural production, which can be traced back to a range of international cultural influences ushered in by colonialism, imperialism, and the Chinese flight from the PRC in 1947. It is precisely this rich array of cultural mixing that is responsible for the melodic and thematic sophistication of Taiwan's pop, which has made it such a success in Chinese-speaking Asia.

1932: The Birth of Taiwan's Pop Music

Taiwan's first exposure to Western musical training began during Dutch colonial rule[4] in 1638, when forty-eight male students began their studies in a Dutch music school.[5] In the late nineteenth and early twentieth centuries, Western missionaries established educational institutions in Taiwan ranging from elementary schools to colleges.[6] Missionaries would continue providing musical education throughout most of the Japanese colonial era (1895–1945).

Japan's educational system also included Western musical theory, which created new musical combinations, such as Japanese-style music using Western instruments in Taiwan.[7] Western-style musical groups performed through most of the Japanese colonial era,[8] and music imported from China contributed to this already complicated mix.[9]

The mass production of Taiyupop (Hokkien dialect pop music in Taiwan) was directly linked to the film industry, getting its start in 1932 when interpreters narrated the dialogue during silent movies.[10] In that same year a 1931 Shanghai film with the unforgettable title *The Peach Blossom Weeps Blood* (*Taohua qixieji*) was released in Taiwan. To accompany the movie, a Taiwanese lyricist used the melody of an old folk song with new Hokkien lyrics to create what is widely recognized as Taiwan's first pop song.[11] Bearing the same name as the movie it was created for, the success of the song "The Peach Blossom Weeps Blood" inspired Shojiro Kashiwano, chairman of the Japanese-run Taiwan branch of Columbia Records, to produce a series of other singles in 1933.[12] Columbia Records made more than 3,500 Hokkien albums in the Japanese colonial period.[13]

In 1935, Japan's Victor Records also began recording Taiyupop songs as well as Hokkien folk music and quickly became Columbia Records' main competitor.[14] Within a year, several other Taiwanese record companies also began producing both Mandarin and Hokkien pop records.[15] In its initial stages, Taiyupop, like

Figure 3. A Western-style band in Taiwan during the Japanese colonial era (1895–1945). The men are wearing Western suits and ties while the women are dressed in Japanese fashion so that imperialism and colonialism are inscribed in their clothing in very gendered terms.

Chinese-language popular music of the time, was a mixture of Western instruments and the extremely high-pitched singing style of Peking opera. Indeed, Columbia Records' most famous singer, Chun Chun, was a trained Peking opera singer.[16]

In the 1930s Taiwan's literary movement already had a strong influence on Taiyupop lyrics.[17] "Facing the Spring Breeze" is an excellent example of the poetic expression in such songs.

FACING THE SPRING BREEZE
She sits alone under the lamp
with the cool breeze in her face.
Sixteen or seventeen
and still unwed
she waits for a young man.
Just as she had hoped
he is handsome and of fair complexion.
What family is he from?

She longs to ask but is too shy
and her heart beats so fast.

If "The Peach Blossom Weeps Blood" was the first Taiyupop song to evolve out of a movie, "Facing the Spring Breeze" can be said to be the most popular.[18] Indeed, this song was cited by many of those I interviewed as the most important pop song in Taiwan's history.[19] "Facing the Spring Breeze" nicely highlights the theme of a passive woman waiting for a man—an issue that I will explore in detail in chapters 4 and 5. The restrained nature of the romance—suggesting the excitement of an arranged marriage, no less—marks it as music from a different age. Couching the theme of this song in terms of anticipation cleverly avoids tainting the woman as promiscuous (at that time simply being seen alone with a man would taint a woman) while still evoking the nervous excitement of romantic interest.

As opposed to the KMT policies that would come later, the Japanese government was quite tolerant of the presence of Taiyupop for most of its colonial rule of Taiwan. It was only on July 7, 1937, when Japan invaded China, that Japan ushered in an era of intense militarism in Taiwan. In 1941, Japan's colonial administration forbade Chinese-language songs,[20] and both love ballads and pop songs were promptly replaced by patriotic military songs.[21]

In the 1930s it was common to take melodies from mainland China and to reproduce them with Hokkien lyrics.[22] Extending this tradition, in 1941 the Japanese government took the melodies from Hokkien and Mandarin Chinese pop songs and added Japanese lyrics as propaganda to recruit Taiwanese men to fight for the Japanese army.[23] Songs that were originally about love and romance were transformed into marches designed to boost popular morale.[24]

1945 to 1949: The KMT's Arrival

When Japan lost the Second World War in 1945 it was forced to cede Taiwan to China as part of the treaty. Taiwan inherited much of mainland China's pop culture as Republican Chinese troops fled to Taiwan from Shanghai and other locations in 1949, but for the next twenty years Hong Kong's music industry, which housed the majority of Shanghai's former songwriters, dominated the Chinese-language pop music market.

In the period between the time the Japanese left Taiwan and the KMT had fully established itself, Taiyupop re-emerged.[25] In the 1960s, Mandopop quickly became aligned with state-controlled television, and Taiyupop continued to be promoted through the medium of films and theatrical performances.[26] In the 1970s the KMT began passing laws against the use of Hokkien lyrics in songs.[27]

Through overt censorship or government subsidies, Taiwan's government main-tained a strict control on mass media until the early 1980s,[28] and Taiyupop only re-emerged in state-regulated mass media after martial law was lifted in 1987.[29]

1977 to 1981: Campus Songs

In 1977 Sony Music introduced the Golden Melody Awards, aimed at recruiting singers and composers from the ranks of university students in order to boost sales in that market.[30] This took the form of "campus songs" (*xiaoyuan gechu*)—folk songs that were written and performed by university students during the period between 1977 and 1981.

From the 1950s to the mid-1970s Taiwan's pop music unabashedly imitated Western music.[31] It was only in 1979, when the United States switched its politi-cal allegiance from Taiwan to the PRC, that Taiwan's youth started to consciously strive to create their own brand of folk music as a protest against American hege-mony.[32] Yet, although campus songs professed to be a break from U.S. musical trends, one should not forget that they embraced folk music at the same time that folk songs were popular in the United States. The thematic distinctiveness of the music therefore had more to do with focusing on Taiwan's musical and poetic tra-ditions than establishing a completely new genre, as it claimed.

The campus songs movement arose at a highly politicized time in which many Taiwanese felt abandoned by the United States' shift in recognition from Taiwan to the PRC. As a result, campus songs were nationalistic in tone.[33] The question remains, however, as to which nation. Most Taiwanese today view cam-pus songs as a symbol of a quintessentially Taiwanese musical movement. But this revisionist history loses sight of the fact that the music was created with the explicit endorsement of the pro-Chinese KMT government. Indeed, the Mandarin Chinese campus songs were born in the context of larger politics that aggressively promoted Mandarin Chinese in the school system, television broadcasting, and other spheres and overtly discriminated against the majority of Taiwan's citizens, who primarily spoke Hokkien. The content of campus songs, with titles such as "I Am Chinese" (Wo shi Zhonguoren), also spoke of a greater Chinese identity that professed to link China, Hong Kong, and Taiwan as one unified culture.[34]

Campus songs' reliance on university students promoted the music to college-aged listeners and also drew on images of college students' innocence.[35] This in turn helped to promote the idea of a healthy and idealistic society.[36] Indeed, the colleges themselves represented an idyllic utopia, separate from the worldly con-cerns that troubled the nation.[37]

Even today, there is a widespread image of this genre as being free of com-mercial interests. Yet in many ways the music was commodified at its inception—

the movement began with Sony Records' creation of the Golden Melody Awards, after all. By the late 1980s, two corporations (Rock Records and UFO Records) dominated record production in Taiwan; it was in this setting that campus songs became unabashedly commercialized and began to evolve into contemporary Mandopop.[38]

The commercialization of campus songs in the 1980s bled the genre of its more overt political orientation.[39] It also shifted the focus away from songs that tended to express love through metaphors such as "wind, moon, and sea" to more direct expressions of love.[40] As with earlier musical trends in Taiwan, campus songs often adopted poetry for their lyrics,[41] which helped lay the groundwork for the strongly poetic nature of today's Mandopop.

Contemporary Taiyupop

Whereas campus songs and Mandopop are the domain of Taiwan's youth, Taiyupop's fans have traditionally been associated with rural areas, the poor, and the elderly.[42] For many people in Taiwan, Mandarin Chinese is a second language, and it is common to hear people say that Mandarin Chinese is a better language to convey thoughts but that Hokkien is a better language to express one's feelings. Given this sentiment, it is perhaps surprising that songs performed in Hokkien are not more popular among urban youth.

The most obvious reason for this is the difficulty of developing an urban fan base given the history of KMT hostility to the Hokkien dialect until the lifting of martial law in 1987. Also, Taipei, as the capital of Taiwan, is populated not only by native Taiwanese but also by people who came from mainland China in 1949 and their offspring, as well as by Hakka and people from several aboriginal tribes who do not speak Taiwanese as a first language. Because of this, there are many people in Taipei who speak little or no Hokkien. As Mrs. Lu, a thirty-year-old graphic artist in Taipei, points out, the underlying tensions in the growing Hokkien movement, of which Taiyupop is an important component, is far more complex than it first seems.

> I don't like Hokkien songs because I'm not ethnically Taiwanese [*Minnanren*]. I'm Hakka and I grew up speaking Mandarin Chinese. [. . .] No one sings Hakka songs—our population is too small. So songs are all in Mandarin or Hokkien.[43]

Lu's statement problematizes the DPP's assertion that using Hokkien is an innately emancipatory act against Chinese hegemony. Instead, her statement seems to suggest that in many ways the use of Mandarin is less divisive for ethnic minorities in

Taiwan. This, in turn, points to the more expansive reach of Mandarin-language songs. Mandopop can be sold to Chinese-speaking communities in diverse countries such as China, Hong Kong, Singapore, Taiwan, and the United States—something the Taiyupop industry could never hope to compete with. In addition to the enormous sales potential, this creates an image of transnationalism and modernity that is reinforced by the combined economic might of these different countries' music industries, which in turn creates an appeal for youth.

The melodic style and thematic content of Taiyupop are also extremely important here, for Taiyupop has tended to work with established genres from forty years ago and earlier. Contemporary Taiyupop continues to be heavily influenced by the Japanese musical style known as *enka*, for example—a point that Taiwanese are very much aware of.[44]

In turn, Taiwan's Mandopop has been dramatically influenced by Taiyupop in its famed melancholy, or, as Christine Yano says of *enka*, "produced tears for sale."[45] Yet an important dividing line between Taiyupop and Mandopop is that Taiyupop, following the lead of *enka*,[46] is thematically rural, focuses on working-class concerns, and is often nostalgic for an idyllic past.[47] In contrast, Mandopop

Figure 4. Wu Bai is commonly referred to as the godfather of both Taiyupop and Taiwan's rock. Photo courtesy of Edith Chen.

is urban, speaks to middle- and upper-class experiences, and is almost exclusively focused on the present. Therefore, listening to pop music in Taiwan aligns the listener on several axes: Mandopop vs. Taiyupop, young vs. old, urban vs. rural, global vs. local, modernity vs. tradition, and middle class/elite vs. poor.

In the past ten years there have been some surprising developments concerning Taiyupop and its audience. Beginning in the mid-1990s, Hokkien lyrics began entering the mainstream Mandopop market. This is not to say that the traditional style of Taiyupop has diminished, but, rather, that it has diversified in recent years. The growing popularity of Hokkien music in Mandopop circles was almost singlehandedly brought about by singer/songwriter Wu Bai.[48] His heavy Hokkien accent when singing in Mandarin Chinese, and his production of Taiyupop with a modern Mandopop rock style (in both melody and lyrics), have made Hokkien music more popular with youth in Taipei than it has ever been. Not coincidentally, the increasing popularity of Taiyupop in the late 1990s went hand in hand with a growing "Taiwanese" identity as formulated in the cross-Strait political realm of the same period. Wu Bai's use of Taiwanese, then, became an expression of self that many people in Taiwan could identify with in the context of larger sociopolitical shifts.[49]

As an extension of this trend, in the past few years, Hokkien can also be found in Taiwan's hip-hop lyrics. Taiwanese performer Chang Cheng Yue had the following to say about this:

> Hip-hop uses a lot of Taiwanese. This is because with hip-hop you can really say whatever you are thinking. You don't have to be a professional, you can just say it. And the listener can identify (*gongming*) with this. So young people want to find their Taiwanese identities, to discover who they are. So hip-hop uses a lot of Hokkien. This works really well with Hokkien songs. In Taiwanese society today everyone has this feeling. If you go to central or southern Taiwan almost everyone speaks Hokkien. In that environment, where everyone is speaking Hokkien, you will feel especially close (*qinqie*).[50]

Chang Cheng Yue emphasizes the closer emotional impact of Hokkien and the feeling of solidarity and national identity that it produces. Several people I interviewed also suggested that Mandarin words, which tend to be one or two syllables, do not provide the necessary rhythmic flexibility that Taiwanese offers. There is also the possibility that Hokkien is more suitable for social critique than the state-enforced Mandarin Chinese and that Hokkien aligns the singer as ethnically oppressed by virtue of historical governmental antagonism toward the Taiwanese language and people.

Figure 5. Chang Cheng Yue is known for his exceptionally wide range of melodic styles. Photo courtesy of George Trivino.

Aboriginal Music

In addition to the dialogue between Taiyupop, Taiwan-produced Mandopop, and traditional Chinese, Japanese, and U.S. musical influences on Taiwan pop, aboriginal sounds are also sometimes incorporated into Taiwan's Mandopop. This too was spurred on by foreign influences. Enigma's 1994 song "Return to Innocence" featured the singer Difang Duana (Guo Yingnan) from the Puyuma aboriginal tribe in Taiwan. This song gained worldwide popularity and was used in the 1996 Atlanta Olympic Games.[51] Aboriginal music attracted international recognition through Enigma's song and since then has received a great deal of attention in Taiwan. In part it is another component of a larger DPP policy shift to highlight aboriginal culture in order to emphasize Taiwan's identity as distinctive from the PRC.

Quite often the aboriginal imagery in Mandopop has as much to do with racial determinism as with an appreciation of the music itself, however. As an example of this, Ms. Meng, a thirty-one-year-old woman who works at a modern art museum in Taipei, said:

> I prefer aboriginal songs to Mandopop. Aboriginal singers have better voices. It's like black people in the U.S., you know? They have better rhythm.
>
> I don't like Mandopop because it's all talking about love and stuff like that—I don't know, maybe I'm too old for that kind of thing now. Aboriginal songs are about nature and things like that—it is really much more interesting.[52]

Ms. Meng's alignment of aboriginal singing abilities with the performers' "innate natures" highlights the racism that is often embedded in praise of aboriginal music.

In actuality, aboriginal music has little presence in Taiwan's mainstream musical scene. To the degree that it does appear, it has been incorporated as a set of symbols to be used in Chinese-language songs created by Taiwanese performers. Sometimes, as with Bobby Chen's song "Happy Reunion" (Huanju ge), this is in the name of social harmony. At other times, as with Jay Chou's song "Terraced Field" (Titian), they are used to represent traditional Taiwan as part of a larger critique. In yet other instances, aboriginal images are merely visual fetishes that are devoid of content.[53]

1980 to Today—Frayed Borders: Modern Mandopop and its Pan-Asian Audiences

Though contemporary Mandopop shares a poetic sensibility with earlier forms of popular music in Taiwan, it has its own set of distinctive characteristics. Today's Mandopop is more restrained about the expression of physical desire than many 1930s lyrics but it is far more direct than the campus songs era in addressing issues of love and heartbreak. Also, the political nuance of campus songs has shifted to a focus on individual relationships in contemporary Mandopop. Some might find this depoliticizing of pop to be an example of the ways the music has been trivialized through its commercialization. Yet to the degree that pop has been politically subverted in the past thirty years, it has been by self-censorship rather than intrusion from the state—love songs simply sell better and this dictates the shape of musical innovation.[54] This music set the stage for today's pop—a mix of Western and Chinese pop music with a healthy dash of Japanese influences thrown in for good measure. I would suggest, therefore, that Mandopop more directly links to people's lived experiences and hopes and gives a wonderful insight into the shifting concerns of women and men in modern Taiwan.

Before Hong Kong's return to China in 1997, its music was associated with sophisticated cosmopolitanism, in large part because of its thriving economy but also because of its sophisticated movie industry. Even today Hong Kong's movie industry propels its stars to become Mandopop stars, and Mandopop singers easily enter the Hong Kong film industry. This symbiotic relationship helped to maintain the appeal of the Hong Kong Mandopop industry. Hong Kong's Mandopop and music industries also led the way for international coproduction. In the case of Mandopop, many of Hong Kong's best hits employed lyricists from Taiwan because people speak Cantonese in Hong Kong.

Before Hong Kong's return to China in 1997 the dubbing of Hong Kong movies was done with a Taiwan accent. Thus, even something as benign as dubbing introduced Taiwan's more *wenrou* accents to the PRC. On its return to the PRC, however, Mandarin dubbing of male voices in the movies has taken on the deeper, more resonant masculine tone of Beijing, while women's voices often retain their Taiwan *wenrou* inflection. Films such as the musical *Perhaps Love* (*Ruguo Ai*), for example, featured actors from the PRC, Hong Kong, Korea, and an actor from Taiwan whose father is Japanese. The movie's soundtrack features Mandopop songs by each of these performers. After Hong Kong's repatriation to the PRC, audiences in both the PRC and Taiwan turned first to Japanese, and more recently to Korean, pop music[55] to supplement their Taiwan pop.

Koichi Iwabuchi asserts that pop culture is a "soft co-optic power" or an "invisible colonization," and he presents the emergence of Japanese pop as an important opposition to American pop's hegemonic dominance.[56] Given Japan's colonial past, there is, of course, the question of how much of an improvement this is over American hegemony. Yet with regards to music produced in Hong Kong, Malaysia, Singapore, and Taiwan, we see that the production of soft power is indeed a victory for politically marginalized parts of Asia—both countering the PRC's political influences as well as Japanese and American pop hegemony.

Unlike Hong Kong cinema, which is increasingly marketed to both Chinese- and English-speaking audiences, Mandopop is specifically bound to the Chinese-speaking audiences living in Asia and in other areas of the world. In much of East Asia the local and the transnational are fluid, overlapping spheres.[57] In the case of Taiwan pop, the local is created by the transnational through the dissemination of CDs, KTV, and music videos. In a sense, this shared popular culture between

Chinese-speaking nations lends support to the notion of a greater China,[58] or at least for a shared cultural space for Chinese speakers throughout the world.[59] Yet at the same moment it constantly fragments into distinctive local entities that are situated in local political economies and cultures.[60] Thus, as Roy Shuker suggests, global homogenization in music reveals itself as a "cross-fertilization of local and international sounds" rather than the homogenizing force that it might first appear to be.[61]

Rather than holding to national borders, many elite in East Asia increasingly seem to be adopting transnational identities that are connected through large cosmopolitan centers such as Hong Kong, Shanghai, and Taipei.[62] For the majority of Taiwanese who cannot afford such international lifestyles, however, identity is firmly rooted in Taiwan. Yet, although national borders are not disintegrating for this majority, urban borders are. Increasingly, Taiwan seems like one large urban sprawl, and if the smaller cities or villages do not produce transnational pop, they certainly consume it in a similar manner to those living in Taipei. Hybrid identities are thereby constructed in these areas as people from across Taiwan migrate to Taipei, go abroad to work or study, or use music, movies, and fashion as overt markers of being part of cosmopolitan modernity.

This does not mean that rural or traditional cultures have disappeared. Rather, rural lifestyles have been incorporated into the suburbs and backstreet alleys of the cities themselves. Many, if not most, of Taiwan's people leave a "traditional" style home or neighborhood to work or shop in urban cosmopolitanship, only to return to traditional community and family structures at the end of the day.

Part of this disintegration of borders can be seen in the musical relationship between Taiwan and Hong Kong. Chen A-Guai, a lyricist and composer for Taiwan's superstar A-mei (Zhang Huimei), among others, asserts, "You can't separate pop music from Taiwan and Hong Kong—there is just too much overlap between the two."[63]

Miss Luo and Mr. Onion, twenty-four-year-old interior designers in Taipei, disagree with this sentiment, however. When I asked them what they thought of Hong Kong pop, they said:

[Mr. Onion:] Hong Kong's music is much closer to Taiwan's because we work together a lot in creating songs. But they are not exactly the same. Hong Kong's music tends to be faster and the performers are more flamboyant. Taiwan's singers like slower songs and the performers are more down to earth.

[Miss Luo:] Ya, like David Tao [an American-born Chinese performer in Taiwan]. He did a performance where he just sat and played on an acoustic guitar—a Hong Kong performer would never do that![64]

Indeed, the distinctive nature of each region's pop (the PRC as opposed to Taiwan, for example) accentuates important differences to people listening to the music. Taiwanese Mandopop star Valen Hsu elaborates on this point.

> Hong Kong is a good model for music production. Their artists are trained to do everything—they sing and they act. There is a very impressive versatility there. [. . .] Hong Kong and Taiwan music overlap but they are not the same. Hong Kong's songs tend to be cut from the same pattern. For example, Li Yihuang took several of Hong Kong's biggest hits from 2004 and 2005 and merged them to produce one song. It was a great idea and the result sounded good. But you couldn't do that with Taiwan's songs— our songs have more variety in that each song has its own lyrical and melodic style—so they wouldn't blend so well. I think this shows the limited range of Hong Kong's pop music in contrast to the much more expansive range of Taiwan's pop music.[65]

Valen Hsu highlights some of the differences between Hong Kong and Taiwan Mandopop, emphasizing Hong Kong's connection with its movie industry and what she sees to be Taiwan's greater musical range. Mandopop songs also have very different political and social significance to Chinese-speaking listeners from other countries. The emotional valance is analogous to the experience of someone from Australia or England when watching a Hollywood movie. They share a common language and many cultural values, yet there is still something profoundly foreign about the film to these audience members. As I noted in the previous chapter, the mainland Chinese love of Gang-Tai pop is intrinsically a political choice that both symbolizes modernity and emphasizes a desire to transcend China's borders.[66] In contrast, listening to the same music in Taiwan has more of a sense of home. This, in turn, is experienced differently by people in Hong Kong, Malaysia, Singapore, or by Chinese and Taiwanese diaspora throughout the world, with a range of different nuances added by particular cultures, dialects, and ethnic diversities in those locales.

Yet if the experience of listening to these songs varies from region to region, it is also a reminder of commonalities of language and culture, creating a sense of what George Lipsitz has referred to as "diasporic intimacy."[67] Indeed, Mandopop crosses national boundaries in unexpected ways. Tim, an American who lived in Taipei in the late 1990s, told me about his Caucasian American co-worker at a Chinese restaurant in Arizona. His colleague began working at a Chinese restaurant in Spain and said that he had a strong sense of *deja vu* because he recognized all of the Mandopop songs he had heard in Arizona.[68]

Xiangyu, a twenty-six-year-old graduate student in Taipei, sees this internationalization as resulting in the decline of Taiwan's Mandopop, while at the same time she reveals a marked appreciation for the results of such cross-fertilization.

> Japanese and Korean songs are very popular once they use Chinese lyrics for the songs. So a lot of people say that the quality of Taiwan's songwriting has really fallen since the nineties. No one writes good songs anymore— they just take melodies from other countries. [. . .] There are whole collections of adopted songs from other countries that are performed by Taiwanese performers. [. . .]
>
> In Taiwan it doesn't matter if a singer is from Malaysia, Singapore, or Hong Kong. Performers from these places can be very famous—they just need to speak Chinese. [. . .] Even love songs from Thailand are sung in Chinese. It's a lot of fun! They write Chinese lyrics for melodies from their own countries and for them and for us it is a new sound.[69]

Xiangyu highlights the richly diverse border crossing of Asian melodies that are localized by adding Mandarin Chinese lyrics as well as the more sophisticated set of sounds created by drawing on several different cultural traditions. Taiwan's relationship with Japan forcefully demonstrates this point, for in addition to shaping Asian pop culture on its own terms, Taiwan has also become a springboard for Japanese pop culture to reach the transnational Chinese-speaking audience in countries such as China, Hong Kong, and Singapore.[70]

In many ways Taiwan is a testing ground for a musician's worth. As in 1930s Shanghai, musical experience in contemporary Taiwan not only heightens a musician's status at home but exposes him or her to a wider range of musical influences. Taiwan therefore becomes a breeding ground for creative musical innovation both within its borders and beyond.

Stefanie Sun's song "Black Sky" (Tian hei hei) is a good example of the ways such songs cross national borders.

BLACK SKY (Tian hei hei)
[The underlined portion is sung in Hokkien. The rest of the lyrics are in Mandarin Chinese.]

Wo de xiao shihou	When I was little
chaonao renxing shihou	and making a racket because I was headstrong and in an uncontrollably bad mood
wo de waipo cong hui chang ge hong wo.	my grandmother (*waipo*)[71] would always coax me with a song.
Xiatian de wu hou	During summer afternoons

laolao de ge anwei wo	my grandmother's songs would comfort me
na shou ge hao xiang zhe yang	those songs were sung a lot like this:
chang de:	

[Chorus 1] *Ti ou ou, bei luo hou.*	[Chorus 1] <u>Pitch black sky, falling rain.</u>
Ti ou ou.	<u>Pitch black sky.</u>
Luo hou.	<u>Falling rain.</u>

"Black Sky", includes the comforting lyrics that the speaker's grandmother sung in the Hokkien dialect that were taken from an old Taiwanese folk song bearing the same name. Though the original song's lyrics have little bearing on Stefanie Sun's version, the older song was used as a melody to sing to children and thus it highlights a sense of nostalgia for her childhood. Yet Stefanie Sun is from Singapore, not Taiwan. We are therefore witness to a Singaporean performer singing a song that Taiwanese audiences readily interpret as representing Taiwanese lives—transforming it, with very little effort, to represent Taiwanese nostalgia.

Stefanie Sun's 2002 remake of Qi Yu's 1979 song "Olive Tree" (Ganlanshu) is another example of this. The lyrics for this song were taken directly from a poem written by Taiwanese poet and novelist San Mao. Singaporean Stefanie Sun's cover of the song bridges both space and time—again, reliving someone else's history, someone else's past. Thus, as Arjun Appadurai points out, mass media teaches us to long for a past that never existed by "rummaging through imagined histories."[72]

In fact, Stefanie Sun has so successfully entered the Taiwan market that she is the only performer who is both from another country and residing outside of Taiwan whom most Taiwanese continue to think of as producing "Taiwan pop." When I interviewed her, she rejected this notion, however, saying, "I am of course grateful that Taiwan appreciates my songs, but I am from Singapore so I am definitely a Singaporean performer."[73]

Thus, borders are simultaneously created and dispersed in this musical environment. The perception of nationality becomes quite porous—as in the case of Stefanie Sun's work—while still emphasizing differences in both cultural production and reception.

The Adoption and Adaptation of Western Pop

Foreign influences on Chinese music date back to the fifth century AD[74] and have had long-lasting effects that can be seen even today.[75] As I have already noted, multinational capital has also been present since the beginning of the "modern" music industry in China in the beginning of the twentieth century. Addressing the ways in which American, and to a lesser degree European and Latin American, melodies are reproduced with Chinese lyrics is important because Mandopop has so clearly been inspired by Western music. Also, because Western pop differs from Mandopop more dramatically than Mandopop does from pop produced in the rest of Asia, the ways songs are transformed to meet local needs is correspondingly more evident.

Westerners tend to sum up Asian pop music as a mirror of Western identities, with the West at the top of the transnational hierarchy.[76] Eric Thompson asks the important question for Malaysian pop music, however: If it is merely an imitation of the Western form, why would anyone listen to the local versions? In other words, if this is the case, "Why does the 'copy' appeal more to Malay youth than 'the real thing'?"[77] Culture flows in all directions, so the West as an omnipotent hegemony might have more to do with a self-aggrandizing fantasy of the West than a tangible unilateral force.[78]

Western popular culture certainly ushers in foreign values to Asia, yet one should not overlook the ability to transform that power by converting the foreign forms into local models. Asian localization of U.S. cultural production has occurred with Disneyland, Kentucky Fried Chicken, McDonald's, Mickey Mouse, sports, and hip-hop,[79] among others. Similarly, Western material goods in Asia carry a wide range of symbols—class status, individualism, independence, and gender equality—but these meanings are not necessarily synonymous with their original meanings.[80] Eric Thompson explores the ways in which Malaysian pop both embraces "American style love" as inherently associated with modernity, and at the same time rejects it for its selfish individualistic fickleness.[81] Similarly, Homi Bhabha and Michael Taussig examine mimesis as subverting colonial power by metamorphosing it to meet indigenous needs.[82] They argue that although mimesis overtly appears as imitation, it undermines that authority through adopting it to one's own needs, transforming it from what it once was.[83]

The prevalence of English words in Mandopop attests to the high status of Western symbols in Asia, but it is important to keep in mind that Western music is incorporated into a specific set of pre-existing local aesthetics.[84] Mandopop often employs English words in ways that would not be appropriate in the West—the name of the group Kissy (Mixue Weiqi), for example. Michelle (Mixue) and Vickie (Weiqi), the members of this group, provide an additional twist on this in that their Chinese names are transliterations of their English names—in other words, their performing identities began with their English names and were then converted into Chinese.

Indeed, as the grammar and nuances of English terms in these songs shift, it might be better to refer to them as "English inspired words."[85] Also, as Guy De Launey notes for Japan, using too many English lyrics in a song can be intimidating for non-native speakers who have spent years studying a language but have not mastered it.[86] De Launey calls this an "English allergy," which problemetizes the idea that English is an unambiguous set of positive images in Asian countries.[87] Thus, most Mandopop stars tread a thin line between being too Western or not Western enough. Mr. Tao, a forty-two-year-old male in Taipei, for example, dismisses Jay Chou's music as being too Western:

> I don't like Jay or the other pop music being produced today—it is too Western. I prefer pop music from ten years ago because it had more of a Taiwanese cultural flavor.[88]

As a part of this contrast we can also look to E. Taylor Atkins' analysis concerning the slippery issue of musical authenticity in Japan's jazz. What he calls "authenticity anxiety" arises as Westerners and Japanese alike explore the tensions between racial determinism (African Americans do it better) and jazz's fundamental aspect of relying on improvisation, which necessitates malleability and innovation.[89] He also suggests that jazz in Japan confirms stereotypes of Japanese imitators vs. Western creators, in that "authenticity" is often defined as doing it like the original,[90] while simultaneously undermining those stereotypes because the music is inevitably transformed to become indigenized.[91] Thus, global and local musical forms merge to create a new third category.[92]

This concern with the line between the imitation of Western music and localized creative impetus very much fits the case of Mandopop, for it overtly uses Western instruments and follows American models in musical trends, music videos, and broadcasting. Yet Mandopop quickly shifts from imitation to innovation—changing the melodies, lyrics, and the presentation of pop stars to fit local aesthetics and cultural concerns. Unlike Japan's instrumental jazz or Hong Kong's visual media, Mandopop's use of Chinese lyrics has the inevitable result that being accepted in the West was never an option. With very few exceptions, Mandopop makes no attempt to pass as "authentic" for a Western audience and thus, in spite of its heavy Western influences, it can be seen to be self-consciously bound to an East Asian identity.

The adoption and adaptation of Western songs is in many ways an extension of musical innovation in any country. "Sampling," for example, in which DJs create new music from elements of old songs, can be seen as an equalizing process in which every song has its own legitimacy.[93] Indigenous musical changes that often appear to be "mistakes" are an essential component for creativity[94] in what has been called "creative misunderstanding"[95] or "creative consumption."[96] Such "mistakes" are not only the basis for musical innovation, but they carry a deeper political valance as the performer transforms the songs to his or her own uses.[97] As George Lipsitz points out, "At times, musicians have to play in ways that are 'mistaken' by one code in order to remain faithful to another."[98] In other words, in transforming foreign pop music to fit Taiwanese and Chinese aesthetics, what first appears to be inept imitation reveals itself to be savvy marketing and creative expression.

For Mandopop audiences, U.S. pop and Mandopop are as distinctive as blues and rock & roll. While some prefer one to the other, most of the people I have spoken with in Shanghai and Taiwan enjoy listening to both—but they will assign particular moods and activities to each. Mandopop fans tend to prefer to sing Mandopop at KTV or listen to it at home, for example, while opting for Western pop music at dance clubs[99] because the upbeat melodies are better suited for dancing and the lyrics are superficial enough that one can just have a good time without thinking about the weightier, more melancholy, issues associated with Mandopop.

Same Melody, Different Message

Taiwanese performers frequently use foreign melodies with new Chinese lyrics. This most commonly includes tunes from Hong Kong, Japan, Korea, and the United States among a wide range of others. In such cases the songs are usually slowed and sung a bit more softly, and in translating the lyrics into Chinese the songs are usually changed to tell a different story. An example of the transformation of Western pop can be seen in Faye Wong's adoption of the Cranberries' song "Dream." Faye Wong was born and raised in the PRC, moved to Hong Kong at the beginning of her musical career, studied music in the United States, and performs songs in Mandarin Chinese with the occasional CD in Cantonese. Below are the lyrics "Dream" by the Irish group The Cranberries, followed by the lyrics from Faye Wong's Chinese cover of the same song.

DREAMS—THE CRANBERRIES
Oh my life
is changing every day
every possible way.
Though my dreams
it's never quite as it seems
never quite as it seems.
I know I felt like this before
but now I'm feeling it even more
because it came from you.
Then I open up and see the person fumbling here is me
a different way to be.

The following lyrics are from Faye Wang's Chinese cover of the above song:

TO STRUGGLE TO BE FREE (Zhengtuo)—FAYE WONG

Shuo zaijian.	Say goodbye.
Dang ai yi cheng huangyan.	That love is already a falsehood.
Jiesu ba bie liulian.	It's over don't be reluctant to part.
Xin yi juan.	A heart is already weary.
Lu yue zou yue yaoyuan.	The longer one walks down this road the longer the road becomes.
Ni de xin yi bu jian.	Your heart is already nowhere to be seen.
Ceng ai de fen bu qing dui cuo.	It is not clear who is to blame for our recently ended love.
Wo yiwei liu de lei hue zhide.	I thought it would be worthy of shedding tears.
Yiwei wo hui kuaile.	[I] thought I would be happy.

The conversion of this song's themes reveals a good deal about what are and are not acceptable lyrics and content in Mandopop. The original song is an optimistic celebration of love. In the Chinese version, however, the theme quickly shifts to more standard Mandopop concerns of heartbreak. Other added elements include the Buddhist themes of escaping resentment, struggling to free oneself from lingering sentiment, and taking refuge in dreams while recognizing that they are only an illusion—these are all recurring themes in the songs I present in chapters 4 and 5.

The adoption and adaptation of Western pop is by necessity politically charged, but this is perhaps more true for the outside analyst than for those listening to the music. Often, the Taiwanese listeners are unaware that the melodies originated in the United States or other foreign countries. Winnie, a twenty-four-year-old insurance agent in Taipei, comments on this point.

For me music is just for fun so I don't pay much attention to music. [. . .]
So I don't notice if they are copying their stuff from U.S. songs.[100]

In a sense, the fact that so many people are unaware that a song is originally American or European attests to the subtle hegemonic power of the West. Yet it also demonstrates that in the process of localization the music's Western origins often become irrelevant.

Those who are aware that a melody has been adopted from the West usually approve of its localization. As Miss Cai, a twenty-three-year-old secretary at a music company in Taipei points out, the prevalence of adopting foreign songs is a necessary and desirable trait of Mandopop.

They change [foreign songs] into Chinese not so much because people don't like English but because they can make it closer to our experiences to make it more relevant to people in Taiwan.[101]

Indeed, most Mandopop fans are not concerned with "authenticity." Rather, the test of a song's worth is the degree to which it can speak to listeners' experiences and concerns. Xiangyu, whom I cited above, emphasizes this point.

English songs are good but the feeling (*weidao*) is not very appropriate in Taiwan, so they change the content when they change the lyrics.[102]

Taiwanese performer Valen Hsu comments on this phenomenon from the perspective of someone producing this music:

I've performed songs with melodies from Tori Amos, Kate Bush, Cat Stevens, and a Swiss group. You have to change the lyrics because you are singing the song in Chinese so the pronunciation must change and there-

Figure 6. Valen Hsu's (Xu Ruyun) album "66 Pohjoista Leveyttä" (Latitude 66 Degrees (Beiwei Liushiliu du) was accompanied by music videos in Helsinki and Rovaniemi, Finland. Photo courtesy of Valen Hsu.

fore the content also changes. For example, Taiwan has a long poetic tradition in its songs, so you get themes like facing the moon. [. . .] International cooperation creates really nice music because you can draw elements from different musical traditions—the end result is much stronger. Most people in Taiwan don't like it if a song is too American, though. We like our own style so we translate the song to be a better fit for Taiwan's hopes and dreams. Most people in Taiwan don't spend too much time thinking about the music, they just like to listen—that's natural right? So my job is to translate such songs to better fit Taiwanese tastes.[103]

Valen Hsu, and many other people I interviewed, emphasized that the lyrical and cultural "translation" of Western pop is not something she stumbled into, but rather is a consciously creative transformation with an aim of making it more amenable to local cultural values.

Conclusion

To fully appreciate the nature of contemporary Mandopop one must look at its historical roots. If today's Mandopop is transnational, it is because Taiwan's pop music was born of transnational capital and culture. If it shares many aspects with Japanese music, this too is because of historical roots in that Japanese music, government, culture, and economics were integral parts of the development of pop music in Taiwan. If Mandopop seems melodramatic to the Western audience, or more poetic than its American counterpart, it is because of cultural traditions that merged in the early twentieth century and evolved in a particular sociopolitical environment. Thus, to know what makes contemporary Mandopop tick, one must come to terms with the precedents that made this musical form possible.

Pop culture in both Taiwan and the PRC can be seen as a hegemonic Western import ushering in ideas of consumerism, individualism, and youth culture. This ties in with a tendency of the English-language press and academia to treat Mandopop as little more than a poorly made counterfeit of the Western variety. Such critiques miss the larger picture, however. Mandopop is no travesty of imitation but a successfully creative collage of representations of the most powerful cultural forces in Asia. American influences, though significant, are only one part of a larger exchange among many nations, including Hong Kong, Japan, Korea, Malaysia, and Singapore, as well as, to a lesser extent, the adoption of melodies from Thailand, the Americas, and several European nations.[104] Thus, as I outlined in the previous pages, Mandopop is part of a multidirectional flow in which American influences are but one part of this transnational sharing.[105] The hyper-hybridity of Mandopop could only have developed in an intensely transnational culture such as Taiwan, in which boundaries of urban/rural, past/present, and outsider/insider are constantly shifting. Paradoxically, it is precisely this hybrid transnationality that defines Taiwan's local culture.

Certainly we should be aware of hidden transformations of thought that are ushered in with pop culture. Nor should we miss the opportunity to celebrate the wonderful diversity and the creativity with which transnational pop culture is adopted and adapted to fit local needs. Perhaps instead of viewing this process as another example of American hegemony that creates world homogeneity, it is therefore more accurate to see these globalized marketing forces as picking and choosing from many options, of which Western music is but one.[106] People in Taiwan can choose between Japanese food, Thai food, or McDonald's in much the same ways that others might. In part this symbolizes internationality, hybrid modernity, and globalism, but sometimes a cigar is just a cigar and Japanese food is just tasty. In the same fashion, someone from Taiwan or the PRC might listen to American rap and then put on a Mandopop CD before watching a movie from France, Hong Kong, or the United States.

The people I interviewed in both Shanghai and Taipei spoke of being able to relate to Mandopop more than U.S. pop, a preference that subverts U.S. hegemony as an intuitive and emotional response rather than addressing the issues analytically. Yet the symbols are there, whether the audience/consumer articulates this or not. Thus I offer emic (local views) and etic (outside views—in this case, Western analysis), and I leave it to you, the reader, to decide where to draw the lines.

CHAPTER 4

Message in a Bottle

Lyrical Laments and Emotional Expression in Mandopop

I drew away from the window, and sat down in my one chair by the bedside, feeling it very sorrowful and strange that this first night of my bright fortunes should be the loneliest I had ever known.

—Charles Dickens, *Great Expectations*

"You want to tell me about it?" She asked him.
"I don't know. I never have talked about it. Not to a soul. Sang it sometimes, but I never told a soul."

—Toni Morrison, *Beloved*

"Where are the men?" the little prince at last took up the conversation again. "It is a little lonely in the desert."
"It is also lonely among men," the snake replied.

—Antoine de Saint-Exupéry, *The Little Prince*

In spite of the dramatic political liberalization of PRC and Taiwan, their economic growth, and the unprecedented freedom that youth enjoy, there seems to be an increasing sense of loneliness and anomie in both the PRC and Taiwan. Yet emotions such as loneliness, sorrow, and heartbreak are difficult to express in Chinese and Taiwanese cultures, which idealize stoic endurance and emphasize indirectness as a means to maintaining social harmony. In the following pages I will present interviews that demonstrate the ways in which Mandopop songs become a conduit through which people in China and Taiwan can come to understandings of, and express, their own experiences. Mandopop's songs of sorrow serve an array of social functions. One can share a song with a friend to show understanding and sympathy, one can listen to gain comfort from the thought of others sharing one's experiences, and one can go to KTV to sing what cannot be said. Mandopop's seeming superficiality thereby reveals itself to be a surprisingly sophisticated poetic expression that reminds the listener of his or her humanity and helps overcome the social and personal challenges of expressing emotions that, after all, make us human.

Loneliness and Isolation in Taiwan

Durkheim's analysis of anomie as arising from an excess of opportunity leading to a loss of moral authority fits the case of Taiwan well. Urbanization and the breakdown of community as well as familial and religious authority, combined with a growing capitalist infrastructure, have in some sense been liberating, but they have also left many feeling isolated, lonely, and unsatisfied. In one study, for example, an average of 12.3 percent of people living in the cities of Kaohsiung, Taipei, and Taizhong reported that they felt a sense of loneliness or "emptiness"—accounting for an estimated 1.07 million people across Taiwan.[1]

Because of traditional views of gender relations, many women lose contact with their friends when they get married[2] and are lonely as a result.[3] Indeed, Taiwanese women's views of marriage are at an all-time low; it is commonly thought that women get stuck at home with their children while men are out gallivanting around with other women.[4] As a result, many Taiwanese women are choosing divorce or not to marry at all. In 2001, for example, 20 percent of women between the ages of thirty and thirty-four were unmarried,[5] a statistic that would have been unthinkable even a decade earlier. Taiwan also has the highest divorce rate in East Asia,[6] with one new divorce for every 2.53 new marriages.[7]

Women's views of their natal ties are often equally bleak. Anru Lee's study of working-class women in Taiwan demonstrates that although Confucian thought portrays individual subjugation to the needs of the group as part of a desirable order of the cosmos, daughters often resent the sacrifices they make for natal kin that consider them to be part of their husbands' families and will later give all inheritance to their sons.[8] Thus, for many women, filial piety is seen as an irresistible force to be fulfilled rather than to be enthusiastically embraced.[9]

Scott Simon's study of female entrepreneurs highlights more hopeful transitions for women with more economic power in Taiwan,[10] but many of the women he interviews demonstrate a marked cynicism toward community, familial relations, or friendship. In several of the accounts, women relate that they discovered that they had to rely on themselves with statements such as "neither friends nor enemies are eternal"[11] or "but in the end, every individual is alone [. . .] human life is by nature solitary"[12]—opinions that are echoed in Chinese-language scholarship.[13]

Mandopop's concern with loneliness and isolation in many ways reflects the speed with which Taiwan has transformed from a rural agrarian society to an urban industrial environment. In 1949 slightly less than 25 percent of Taiwan's population lived in cities with a population of fifty thousand or more[14]—by 1988 this percentage had risen to approximately 70 percent.[15] Unlike Americans, several generations of whom have dealt with urban capitalism and the strain on familial and community relations that ensued, Taiwanese people in their twenties and thirties were raised on their parents' and grandparents' stories of rural childhoods that were fully immersed in the social ties of small-town alliances. These rural lives had their own problems—a greater pressure to conform, more vulnerability to gossip and peer pressure, and to some extent a more limited range of life choices. With the exception of newly married brides who changed their natal communities and support networks to that of their husbands,[16] however, the fantasy of escaping the pressures of one's social network was no doubt a far larger concern for most than feelings of loneliness.

In the past decade, there has also been a growing sense of economic uncertainty in Taiwan that has been accompanied by an increasing class division,[17] with an estimated average of seventy thousand people a year entering into poverty.[18] Many feel a greater sense of uncertainty about their economic future than they have in decades,[19] and suicide rates have skyrocketed in the past few years.[20]

Another factor leading to loneliness and isolation in Taiwan is a fear of losing face. Between 50 and 53 percent of people in Taiwan report that they are shy, which places them between American (42 percent) and Japanese (60 percent) respondents.[21] People I interviewed in both the PRC and Taiwan listed loneliness as a major social problem and revealed an extremely prevalent belief that people in China and Taiwan are more shy than people in the West. Linked to this is a growing cultural ethos of individualism in Taiwan, which has resulted in a greater need to rely on oneself, which in turn has led many individuals to question their self-worth.[22]

Alienation, Anomie, and Loneliness in the PRC

The PRC shares many of the concerns that I have just outlined for Taiwan. The PRC's unique governmental structure and the remarkable speed of its cultural transition in the past few decades have added several distinctive aspects to this picture, which I will briefly outline here.

If the early communist era wiped out religious belief for many, the Cultural Revolution eliminated any faith in the government for most. Beginning in 1978, Deng Xiaoping's economic reforms signaling a move toward capitalism brought a level of prosperity that has arguably never been seen before in China, but many have been left behind in the transition. The PRC was thrust into a market economy seemingly overnight, and people were confronted with the need to transform their identities because of the larger labor market.[23] While welcomed by most, this ushered in an era that many saw as having all of the same problems as before but, in the words of Hao Huang, was "missing [a] socialist conscience."[24] This "loss of the humanist spirit"[25] has left what many Chinese have referred to as a moral vacuum in China. The lack of job security and widespread low wages, combined with the difficulty of finding work after decades of guaranteed employment, created a general feeling that the 1990s were a harsher world than the 1980s.[26] This has been accompanied by widespread resentment of corruption.[27] Tabloids, for example, evince a growing mistrust of the rich as emblematic of a new corrupt culture in which many are being left behind.[28] In such accounts the poor come to represent the dangers of a new society in which state protection and the iron rice bowl have been melted down for the new currency.[29]

The raw size of the population, combined with a dramatic restructuring of the economy, has resulted in a general ethos of survival at any costs—hardly an environment for feeling part of something larger than oneself. Indeed, the gulf between the rich and the poor is a visual presence in urban centers, where one is witness to people sleeping on the street, beggars, and general poverty that, as Gregory Lee has suggested, "the like of which I had only previously seen in films made by communist producers to expose the social evils of old China."[30] In turn, the dreams leading up to the Tiananmen demonstrations for democracy in 1989 have been replaced by a pervasive cynicism. As Hao Huang notes for today's twenty-somethings:

> The official public amnesia surrounding the Tiananmen massacre has engendered a nihilistic public anomie. Activist students and intellectuals are currently regarded as having brought victimization upon themselves through egotism, elitism, and gross miscalculation of the possible outcomes.[31]

Connecting to this is Nimrod Baranovitch's suggestion that part of Beijing rock's declining popularity in the PRC was a post-Tiananmen cynicism about one's ability to change anything.[32] This new ethos, often embedded in Darwinian rhetoric, is a large factor in making Mandopop's themes of loneliness and alienation so relevant to many in the PRC.

Differing Rhetorics and Disappointed Realities

The prevalence of the themes of loneliness and isolation in the PRC and Taiwan is in some sense surprising, yet the range of social pressures that I have reviewed in the preceding pages does seem to suggest that many do indeed feel isolated. An essential factor here is that growing individualism has provided many people with ammunition to protest the greater abuses of traditional familial obligation. While this freedom to rebel is in many ways a good thing, it has created a vacuum that family ties, for better or worse, had once filled.

The growing expression of loneliness and isolation can also be explained, at least in part, by the ideological structures of traditional Chinese and Taiwanese cultures. In the United States, for example, individualist rhetoric is such that a fundamental part of being American is believing oneself to be an individual. In this ideological framework, separation from family or friends in the interest of career is seen as a natural event.[33] To the extent that this leads to ideological conflict, the problem lies in the attempt to explain one's feelings of loneliness when one is doing the "natural" thing—for example, moving to a new city for a promotion, thereby leaving one's family and community behind.[34]

In China and Taiwan, however, Confucian and other indigenous ideological views portray a world in which one's social ties not only define one's identity but are the basis of their social world. Many people in Taiwan, for example, feel that they should not feel lonely because it is unnatural.[35] I would suggest, therefore, that part of the trauma of being alone in China and Taiwan is based on the greater expectation that one should be part of a group.

Mr. Tao, a forty-two-year-old independently wealthy male in Taipei, demonstrates this point:

All people have lonely periods in their lives. In Taiwan people like to get together; it isn't like the U.S. where people like to go home alone. Taiwanese people like to have lots of people around, and they are never alone. It's sort of like when you start drinking and you feel good and you hit a high point and then you get too drunk and you feel really bad. It is the same thing, when you go out with your friends you are really happy but afterwards when you go home you feel even more lonely because of the contrast—after people have left then you are all alone—then what do you get? Sorrow.

Or say someone is driving his car alone. Maybe he has sex or goes out with someone, and then says good-bye and goes home. On the drive back you might enjoy that last moment when you are thinking about it but then you feel more and more by yourself. That's lonely. You want to keep that good feeling—you want it to last longer.[36]

Paradoxically, then, part of the loneliness that people in China and Taiwan feel arises from their greater group orientation. In other words, whereas many in the West might look at the separation from friends and family as an unfortunate but inevitable event, in modern China and Taiwan, individualism has been ushered in by the modern capitalist infrastructure at such a fast pace that it has not yet been naturalized. Part of the problem, then, is for an individual to explain why relationships are not enough, or why they are unfulfilling, when so much of their culture tells them that they are part of a greater whole.

Mandopop as Modern Laments

Given the pressures of the traditional family system, modernization might seem like a liberating force to many. Certainly, the contemporary social trend that empowers the individual at the expense of the group is marketed as an appealing choice by the youth-oriented film and music industries. Yet in the midst of the personal liberation that modernity promised is a sense of anomie and alienation that accompanies it. As outlined above, tragedies of the traditional world are thereby replaced by the Weberian iron cage of the modern one—a fact that is made no easier to bear because people chose this path themselves.

I want to emphasize that my goal here has not been to suggest that people in the PRC or Taiwan are more lonely than in other countries, but rather to demonstrate that there are factors in these societies that cause loneliness, isolation, and anomie to be resonant themes for many. The sorrow expressed in Mandopop can be seen as an eloquent expression of the grief of the age, and in looking at scholarship on other areas of Asia, one gains a sense that the PRC and Taiwan are not alone in this.

The melancholy nature of Mandopop is in part due to the influences of Japanese *enka* and Taiyupop, which are notoriously maudlin, and in part because people in both the PRC and Taiwan are suckers for a tragic ending. This is an extension of similar themes in East Asian movie industries, traditional and contemporary literature, and the wildly popular soap operas produced in Japan, Korea, and Taiwan. This sadness colors Japanese music in Japan ranging from jazz to *enka* to *gunka* war songs.[37] Similarly, it has been suggested that the sorrowful (*beiqing*) tone of much of Japanese literature has had a profound effect on Taiwan's literature,[38] which in turn affects Taiwan's movie and music industries. Chinese television drama focusing on "youthful despair and social ennui" is another example of a prevalent passion for melancholy.[39] In fact, as Wu Jing-jyi has pointed out, loneliness is a prominent theme in all forms of Taiwan's mass media, ranging from literature to soap operas to cinema to popular music.[40]

Miss Yan, a twenty-three-year-old college graduate looking for work in Shanghai, suggests that Mandopop is an eloquent expression of these social tensions:

[In addition to Gang-Tai pop] lyrics in music produced in China also revolve around loneliness (*jimo*) and isolation (*gudu*). Especially in Shanghai, people's lives are very individualistic. You go to work and you have to depend on yourself so you can feel very lonely. I just graduated from university and now all my friends are moving back to their home cities because they couldn't find work in Shanghai. So my whole social network disappeared overnight—that is of course a lonely feeling. So the songs capture this—people's sense that they are losing friends who have to focus on their careers to survive. I think Taiwan's songs, especially, capture this feeling very poetically. I think people in Shanghai can really identify with the lyrics of Taiwan songs.[41]

Miss Dai, a twenty-two-year-old Taiwan university graduate with a degree in economics, emphasizes this point for Taiwan as well:

Many people are lonely in Taipei. Every day they go to work and their faces carry smiles but they are not truly happy. If you have a problem you can't talk about it. [. . .] For example, before I found work I felt lonely but I couldn't talk to anyone about it. I still had to smile when I saw people even though I was very lonely. People can't talk to others about their unhappiness so they listen to songs that make them cry. When I listen to this kind of song I feel like someone understands me and after crying I feel a little bit better.[42]

As Miss Dai points out, the sad nature of Mandopop provides social solidarity that comforts through shared pain. This common ethos is clearly as responsible for the transnational appeal of Mandopop as the linguistic commonality that more overtly links urban centers such as Hong Kong, Shanghai, and Taipei.

Loneliness and isolation are not new themes to Chinese or Taiwanese cultures, but who expresses them, and when they do so, differs. Traditional Chinese poetry was a conduit to express loneliness and isolation, but, unlike Mandopop, this was primarily the domain of the educated elite. Rather than focusing on loneliness resulting from the end of romantic relationships, as is the case with Mandopop, traditional poetry often revolved around the burden of the poet's responsibilities in the political sphere and the isolation that came with his post. In contrast, Mandopop centers on themes of romance and heartbreak and reaches youth in every sector of society.

Mandopop's melancholy is shared with other Asian musical genres such as Japanese *enka* and Taiyupop. Yet it is distinct from these genres in that whereas *enka* and Taiyupop focus on nostalgia, Mandopop is overtly present-oriented. Though occasionally lamenting the loss of past loves or fears of a lonely future, the emphasis of Mandopop lyrics is almost inevitably the pain, or joy, of the moment.

As Jeroen de Kloet points our for Hong Kong, Mandopop's seeming superficiality is a commitment to the moment in that the speed with which pop trends come and go reflects the frenetic pace of urban centers such as Hong Kong,[43] Shanghai, or Taiwan. This fragmented present orientation also accentuates the sense of anomie and alienation that arises in these songs in that they highlight fractured realities rather than expressing a belonging to communities with long-term social and emotional ties.

As with the strong focus on the present, it is anyone's (and everyone's) story, immediately convertible to any urban landscape in the PRC, Taiwan, or beyond. Thus, Mandopop comforts because it suggests that others share these experiences, even if one does not know them. A Mandopop song is therefore akin to a message in a bottle that is sent with an almost desperate hope that it will drift to an unknown destination to send rescue.

Lyrical Laments

In the previous pages I explored the ways in which loneliness and isolation are far more central concerns than one might have expected in the PRC and Taiwan. This is forcefully evinced when examining the prevalence of words for loneliness and isolation in Mandopop lyrics. Looking at a list of twenty top-selling CDs in Taiwan, for example,[44] I catalogued the frequency of key words concerning loneliness and/or isolation, which can be summed up as follows:

jimo	lonely, lonesome	36 times
gudan	alone, lonely, friendless, isolated, solitary	26 times
gudu	lonely, isolated, solitary, alone	13 times
guji	lonely, isolated, desolate	5 times

In total, key words for loneliness and/or isolation appeared 80 times in 227 songs. As a point of contrast, a similar compilation for the top 20 CDs in a U.S. billboard chart for best sales[45] included only 17 words for loneliness or isolation in 306 songs. Also, in all of the U.S. songs the lonely/isolated key words came up as passing references whereas these same terms were usually thematically central to the Mandopop songs.

The actual percentages of lyrics about loneliness in Mandopop charts vary from week to week and are somewhat different according to who is providing the data, but these themes are consistently prevalent from year to year.[46] Also, because it is common to use almost an entire song's lyrics as the chorus—repeating almost all of the lyrics several more times—a listener is often confronted with these key-words far more than is suggested by these numbers. Furthermore, in examining

Mandopop lyrics it soon became clear that the majority of the songs express loneliness even if they do not use the specific vocabulary.

In the next chapter I address gender construction of Mandopop lyrics. The themes of loneliness and isolation are so evident in the songs I examine for that purpose that I will not present sample lyrics of this kind here. I will, however, provide one example of a song that does not contain any of these key words, though it forcefully conveys these sentiments. This song, performed by Wawa, is an excellent example of a song about loneliness that does not use the actual words.

"WANDERER WITHOUT A DESTINATION" (Meiyou zhongdian de liulang)

Yi ju hua.	One sentence.
Liangge ren.	Two people.
Si mian huise de wei qiang.	Surrounded by four gray walls.
Wangle houlai.	[I] forget what happened afterwards.
Ta de yingzong.	The traces that he left [*yingzong*].[47]
Que hai jide dang shi ta chuan guo de chenshan.	But [I] still remember the shirt he wore at the time.
Sheme muyang.	What it looked like.

With most Mandopop, lyrics for loneliness are pervasive, either in the form of feeling lonely or in expressing that one's new love has driven away loneliness.[48] "Wanderer Without a Desitination" never uses the key words for "lonely" or "isolated" but there is a marked contrast between the female speaker surrounded by four walls in a single person's room and the man's wandering freedom that evokes these sentiments equally well.[49] As with many songs of this genre, the woman in "Wanderer Without a Destination" is passive in contrast to the lover, who roams. The use of the first person is almost completely omitted in the above song. The singer is passive as she witnesses events that seem to appear and disappear disjointedly before her eyes. This stream of consciousness highlights the emotional impact of her severed relationship by conveying her utter disorientation. The lyrics jump from two people being trapped in an unpleasant circumstance (One sentence / two people / surrounded by four gray outer walls) to an emphasis of being completely alone, as is demonstrated by these lyrics that I did not include in the above excerpt (One lamp / one dream / remains in a single person's room). Single units of property in a room inhabited by a solitary person create the feeling of isolation that the other songs in this presentation explicitly state. By juxtaposing long, flowing prose with cramped, fragmented phrases, the lyrics convey a feeling of being isolated—both from the outside world and in a sense forcibly detached from her own experiences because her memories are confined to brief, fragmented moments. Thus, the performed emotion is left in seemingly random order and, like abstract art, is jarring because of its disconnectedness. As this song and others demonstrate, the prevalence of the themes of loneliness and isolation are even greater than the explicit use of specific words for these sentiments.

Singaporean performer Stefanie Sun has this to say about why loneliness is such a pervasive theme in Mandopop:

> Loneliness is not really one theme. There are many kinds of loneliness. There is loneliness in a crowd, loneliness when you are alone, loneliness when you are with friends, or with family. There is also loneliness when you have just ended a relationship and loneliness while you are still in a relationship. So one reason this is such an important theme in Mandopop is that it covers such a wide range of emotions and experiences. There is a lot of material there if you want to explore human emotions, which a good song should do. Mandopop songs are very sensitive to this range of experiences and because everyone has gone through these experiences a lot of people can relate to the songs.[50]

Figure 7. Stefanie Sun (Sun Yanzi), Singapore's most successful Mandopop performer, made her career in the Taiwan music industry.

Stefanie Sun emphasizes the range of emotions and experiences conveyed with this seemingly narrow theme. She highlights the fact that one need not be alone to feel lonely, a point that several of the other people I interviewed brought up.

Miss Su, a twenty-eight-year-old Malaysian of Chinese descent, is a television host in Malaysia and bears a remarkable resemblance to Stefanie Sun. She was educated in Chinese schools in Malaysia and feels a certain kinship with Taiwan but also perceives it with an outsider's perspective.

> I think we are all a little unhappy because we have too many choices. So we don't know what we want and that makes people feel unhappy. Taiwanese people are very nice but I think they always want a little bit more. If you tell someone in Malaysia "you can have ten" then they are happy with ten. If you tell someone in Taiwan "you can have ten" they will say "why can't I have fifteen?" This creates a mindset where one is always wanting more, always a little dissatisfied with what one has.[51]

With characteristic humor, Taiwan's performer Chang Cheng Yue also feels that melancholy is part of Taiwanese culture:

Figure 8. Chang Cheng Yue addresses the ubiquitous nature of lonely Mandopop lyrics with characteristic humor. Photo courtesy of George Trivino.

Taiwanese people are extreme (*jiduan*) [they have bigger emotional highs
and lows] they are more sensitive (*mingan*). They might say, "Oh, I'm
so sad" and then a minute later they will say, "Oh, I'm so depressed!
(*beishang*) [so the sadness quickly escalates]."[52]

Physical environment may also play a role here. To Miss Su, whom I quoted above,
Taiwan's dense population, bleak concrete buildings, and relative lack of public
space all play a role in creating an environment of sadness and isolation.[53] George
Trivino, who runs his own record label in Taipei, linked the maudlin melodies of
Mandopop with larger geopolitical themes, referring to Taiwan's weakness both
in its colonial history under Dutch and Japanese rule and under the KMT's rule
beginning in 1949.[54]

In many ways Mandopop successfully captures a rather melancholy side of
PRC and Taiwan culture yet in another sense, in allowing for the expression of
taboo topics, the music allows for a psychological catharsis. PRC scholar Huang
Shusen, who also links loneliness to a physical culture, elaborates on this point:

We live in overcrowded cities with fierce competition. We feel lost and
lonely (*jimo*) and look for ways to rid ourselves of the unbearable sadness,
loneliness (*guli*), and helplessness. [Mandopop love] songs are good
medicine [for these ills].[55]

Miss Guo, a twenty-five-year-old marketing executive in Taipei, also suggests a
positive twist to this seemingly pessimistic environment:

I've never cried at KTV but sometimes at home I'll cry when listening to
a song. Many songs are really beautifully written. [. . .] Taiwan's pop songs
are sad because we all like to feel this way. A lot of times we are so busy at
work we become obsessed with day-to-day tasks. Pop songs and movies
remind us to feel. They remind us of what is important, like love and
caring—these feelings—that is what matters but we often forget because
we're so busy.
      As to why the songs are so sad, we live in a very complex world. The
world changes so fast and you have to be able to adapt. This is not a caring
world but one of survival—life in a big city. So we listen to these songs and
it is a release. That's why I like sad songs sometimes. I feel better after this
kind of release.[56]

Huang Shusen and Miss Guo reframe Mandopop's lonely ethos in a positive light.
This view, echoed by many others I have spoken with, emphasizes that the poetic

expression of despair reminds one of one's humanity in the midst of an urban capitalist environment that transforms people into commodities. Thus, as Christine Yano suggests for the Japanese music genre *enka*, in a strange sense this expression of sorrow is comforting in that it "holds up to public view a communally broken heart."[57]

I'M NOT SAD (Wo bu nanguo)

[Chorus 2] *Wo zhende dong.*   [Chorus 2] I truly understand.

Ni bu shi xixinyanjiu.   You are not the kind to be fickle in affection.

Shi wo meiyou   It was I who was not

pei zai ni shenbian dang   by your side when you were lonely [*jimo*].
     ni jimou shihou.

Bie zai kanzhe wo   Don't look at me anymore

shuozhe ni ai guo.   and say you used to love [me].

Bie tai shangtong.   Don't be too hurt.

Wo bu nanguo.   I am not sad.

Zhe bu suan shenme.   This is a little thing

Zhe shi weishenme yanlei hui liu?   Only, why are my tears falling?

Wo ye bu dong.   I don't understand either.

Maria is a thirty-three-year-old secretary from Tainan. One easily forgets her age because of her active enthusiasm for all manner of things and a rather endearing inability to navigate the streets of her hometown of Tainan without getting lost. She had this to say about the above song in relation to her own life.

> I really like the song "I'm Not Sad" by Stefanie Sun. A friend gave me this song because my situation was the same as the person in the song. So she copied the song to give to me. It really is like my story. [. . .] The girl who gave me the song is a good friend and knows my relationship with a certain guy. I've known this guy a really long time and we were really good friends and always spent a lot of time together talking and such. I told him I liked him and he said he had a girlfriend. Afterwards it was hard to talk to him. He told me how tender [*wenrou*] she was so our relationship could not be. [. . .] The first time I sang the song at KTV I cried. Then I felt better because I knew other people also went through this so I felt better—not so pitiful. I went to KTV to sing this song and it felt like my song, not Stefanie Sun's song.[58]

Maria's statement, "I went to KTV to sing this song and it felt like my song, not Stefanie Sun's song" suggests that people internalize Mandopop lyrics to reflect their own experiences. Two days earlier, when I had casually spoken with Maria about the same song (without pen and paper unfortunately), she told me that it was about a boyfriend who abruptly let go of the singer's hand when he saw his other girlfriend. She revised this account two days later (in the above interview) after she was able to look at the lyrics more carefully—in fact, she downloaded the lyrics from the Internet and brought them to our meeting. Neither version of the song was an exact match for Maria's experiences, however, in that Maria never was romantically involved with her love interest, whereas the song describes a couple that had once mutually been in love.

As David Henderson points out, the success of both poets and musicians can be attributed to their ability to create works that are vague enough that readers and listeners can project their own experiences onto the art.[59] Maria's conversion of the song's meaning points to the flexibility of the music and the creative appropriation of the listeners. The audience's interpretation of Mandopop can therefore be seen as a constantly changing act of translation. This communication is in many ways more effective than a spoken interaction in that the listener can more closely identify with the experience. In allowing the reader to project his or her own experiences onto the lyrics, the lyricist allows for the necessity of translation between conflicting experiences. It should be noted, however, that the songs are also limited by that very fact. In other words, the more the audience projects onto the statement, the more they distort it. The songs therefore become continually shifting dialogues between the lyricists and the listeners.

In our interview, Maria also noted the Buddhist emphasis on mercy and letting things go in the songs.[60] Mrs. Chen, a forty-six-year-old Chinese language teacher in Taipei, also raised this point:

> Song companies know what sells. They don't like songs about resisting fate because people can relate better to putting up with mistreatment. [. . .] Maybe you have an argument with your husband and listen to a song and feel better and forgive him. The other kind of songs are angry, so when you listen to them the problem becomes even worse. So these songs comfort people.[61]

Mrs. Chen sees Mandopop as a means of regaining emotional balance. She uses the music as a way of attaining solace and avoiding confrontation. In listening to songs of forgiveness, therefore, Mrs. Chen recognizes that her problems are not unique, which helps her to smooth over her marital difficulties.

Maria cited prevalent cultural shyness and lack of time as reasons why people feel more isolated in today's Taiwan. Mandopop songs echo this concern, for the prevalent theme of loneliness frequently links to a story of loving someone secretly but not being able to tell him—usually because he is in another relation-ship.[62] Slow, simple melodies accentuate a feeling of loneliness (*jimo*) and isolation (*gudan*) in the songs.[63] Mr. Chen, a thirty-year-old male who works for a cellular phone company in Shanghai, elaborated on these concerns:

> Mandopop songs revolve about being lonely more because Chinese sup-press their feelings more. In Europe people are really open about what they are thinking and feeling, but we tend to cover things up more. That's why we like these songs, because they talk about emotions that everyone has but that we have a hard time expressing.[64]

This point arose in several other interviews as well. Xiangyu, a twenty-six-year-old graduate student in Taipei, said the following:

> [The emphasis on Buddhist forgiveness] is a racial (*minzu*) characteristic. Taiwanese people believe that you should endure (*rennai*) but never say anything, so we listen to songs and cry. Americans express their feelings more easily. If you are lonely or sad in Taiwan you can't talk about it, so you listen to songs that express this feeling. Taiwanese people think a long time before doing things.[65]

These statements point to the prevalence of shyness and introspection in daily life as causing a social isolation that results in loneliness. The difficulty of speaking directly, a modern-day extension of traditional Chinese etiquette, is also a recur-ring theme in their explanation of why loneliness is so common in songs and in people's lives.

If shyness is commonly thought to cause loneliness expressed in song, Man-dopop can also be used as a means of expressing oneself more directly, which provides a safety buffer should one's confession be met with rejection or awkward-ness. Maria noted that friends who feel awkward discussing intimate matters can express understanding and sympathy by exchanging popular songs.[66] Similarly, Miss Fu, a twenty-five-year-old elementary school teacher who moved to Shang-hai to be with her fiancé, said the following:

> It can be very lonely in Shanghai. [. . .] We Chinese like sad stories in general—they are more moving. That is true if you look at movies or television dramas or music. But also I think that songs with lonely lyrics fill a place in our lives because we can't really talk about that with people. So we can go to KTV with a group of friends and select a song that talks

about it—maybe being lonely, maybe having someone break your heart—it is a way of letting people know you have had these kinds of experiences without everyone becoming uncomfortable.[67]

Another example of this sentiment can be seen when Miss Zhou, a twenty-five-year-old Taiwanese woman pursuing a degree in fashion design in England, said:

> Sometimes I'm really sad in England. I remember a song and think "That's exactly like me right now." Also, with songs I can share my feelings with my friends. I can share them with my boyfriend and he will know I really feel sad. It is hard to talk about being sad—your friends or boyfriend will feel uncomfortable because it is too serious a topic. But if you sing it, it doesn't threaten anyone—because otherwise sometimes people don't want to listen. They get scared if you say serious things, so you sing.[68]

These are but a few of the many statements in my interviews that point out that Mandopop songs are a conduit to expressing emotions that are difficult to broach in daily conversation. In Maria's case, a song is exchanged to signify her friend's sympathy and understanding. For Miss Zhou, singing songs of loneliness becomes part of a repertoire to communicate with her boyfriend—and because this is such a common technique, there is little doubt that the boyfriend understood. Miss Fu links the sentiments in Maria and Miss Zhou's accounts by suggesting that the interrelatedness of exchanging songs and performing them is a means of emotional communication.

Conclusion

Mandopop's themes of loneliness and isolation are hammered in by the lyrics and by the pictures that accompany CDs, KTV, live performances, and magazine coverage. Mandopop songs help people feel that they are not alone—that the lyricists, performers, and other audience members share their pain. Audiences use Mandopop's poetics to gain solace, to come to a better understanding of their experiences, and to communicate emotions that are normally discouraged in daily conversation.

Most people I have spoken with in Shanghai and Taipei said they feel that the world around them is crumbling—that a breakdown of traditional moral and religious values is resulting in a moral vacuum. As David Buxton has suggested for the West,[69] consumerism is largely filling this kind of void. Mandopop reaches everyone's lives through consumption in the form of CDs, cinema, KTV, radio, and television. It reflects this consumerist embrace of modernity while simultaneously insisting that we remind ourselves of our own humanity through singing songs of sorrow.

The songs express despair, but they inevitably do so in terms of an absent lover or the performer's own experiences—economics, politics, or other social forces are usually self-censored as part of a marketing strategy. This is in part because Taiwan and Hong Kong's music industries do not want to risk losing the PRC's huge market, but, more importantly, Mandopop fans on both sides of the Taiwan Strait prefer not to think about such matters and tend not to listen to (or buy) politically oriented music.

Thus, in direct contrast to Western stereotypes of the music, Mandopop's melancholy can be seen as an attempt to deal with surprisingly serious issues. It provides a means for people in China and Taiwan to express loneliness, isolation, and anomie more honestly than everyday speech and culture allow. As the old adage goes, "laugh and the world laughs with you, cry and you cry alone," but perhaps Mandopop is an innovative solution to transcend this barrier.

The people I interviewed in Shanghai and Taipei believe that Mandopop's lonely lyrics point to a greater poetic sense and search for meaning than pop in the United States. Thus, rather than viewing the melancholy of Mandopop as revealing negative aspects of China or Taiwan, it may be more accurate to stress that Mandopop's lyrics are evidence of poetic creativity, of careful introspection, of emotional expression denied in everyday conversations, and of reasserting humanity into a seemingly uncaring world.

CHAPTER 5

Men Writing Songs for Women Who Complain about Men

Mandopop's Gender Construction in Taiwan and the PRC

And here it would seem from some ambiguity in her terms that she was censuring both sexes equally, as if she belonged to neither; and indeed, for the time being, she seemed to vacillate; she was a man; she was a woman; she knew the secrets, shared the weaknesses of each.

—Virginia Woolf, *Orlando*

An identity is always already an ideal, what we would like to be, not what we are.

—Simon Frith, *Performing Rites: On the Value of Popular Music*

As we saw in the previous chapter, both Mandopop lyrics and the people I interviewed demonstrate that the expression of loneliness and isolation in urban China and Taiwan is in many ways a highly gendered experience. In this chapter I shift the focus from Mandopop's articulation of women's lives to the ways in which female identities are constructed.

In a Word, Gender

Mandopop is usually a cooperative venture with one person composing the melody, another writing the lyrics, and a third singing the songs. Men also frequently write songs for other male performers, yet though many of the most popular performers are women, the majority of lyricists writing their songs are men. Songs performed by men that are written by women are almost nonexistent.[1] Thus, men write songs for women to sing, complaining about men.

Men have been writing lyrics for women to perform since the birth of the Mandopop industry in 1930s Shanghai,[2] drawing on performative traditions that date back long before that. There tends to be a performer/audience divide in categorizing types of songs, for whereas almost all of the lay people I interviewed defined "women's songs" as being linked to the gender of the performer, the majority of people I spoke with in the music industry emphasized that just because a song is sung by a woman does not mean it is necessarily a woman's song.

In their own distinctive ways, both views suggest that music transcends gender boundaries. In the first case, ignoring the gender of lyricists highlights the constructed nature of gender roles. In the second view, the fact that men and women can sing of the same experiences and emotions highlights the profound similarities of women and men even though the content of such songs is still more often than not bound to remarkably traditional gender typologies.

This is a very different form of gender bending than in traditional Chinese opera[3] or contemporary cinema,[4] in which male actors wear women's clothing or vice versa. For whereas the double readings created in those contexts is something that tends to shock, amuse,[5] or be subversive,[6] "women's songs" are taken to reflect real women's experiences regardless of whether a man or a woman wrote the song. In other words, theater offers cross-dressing as an always acknowledged presence, whereas Mandopop transforms it into a non-issue in which the fact that men write for women is not a statement, but rather a male contribution to seemingly real desires, emotions, and experiences of women.

The people I interviewed in both Shanghai and Taipei conceptualized Mandopop lyrics as being accurate representations of the real world. Lyrics can therefore be seen as relatively accurate poetic representations of listeners' hopes and dreams. For example, studies have found that Taiwan's teenagers have almost identical opinions with Mandopop lyrics regarding the natural characteristics of men and women, conceptions of love, relationships, and breaking up—even when the students had no experience of their own in these matters.[7]

Several scholars have asserted that Mandopop lyrics teach youth how to conceptualize relationships as well as gender identities.[8] Liu Honglin stresses that Mandopop in Taiwan is the most popular among high school and university students—the exact ages when Taiwan's youth begin dating.[9] Because of traditional sanctions against teenage dating, combined with expectations among today's youth that they will do so, teenagers cannot ask for advice from teachers or parents. It has been suggested that as a result Taiwan's youth are even more influenced by love songs' lyrics than are youth in the West.[10]

Although Mandopop lyrics clearly do help shape youths' thoughts and behavior, it would be a mistake to think of Mandopop as a totalizing force. Teleological arguments such as these lose sight of the fact that the lyrics also reflect pre-existing cultural conceptions that adolescents might be getting from cinema, literature, and other forms of mass media, as well as from the statements and behavior of their friends, parents, teachers, and other social relations. Gender differences are also legitimated through the lens of Western science or medicine, which naturalize the conception of women as emotional and men as intellectual, views that have a long history in both China and Taiwan.[11] Thus, Mandopop simultaneously provides models for gendered thought and behavior and reflects pre-existing conceptions of gender. The vast majority of Mandopop songs are about love, approximately half to four-fifths of love songs are about breaking up,[12] and almost 80 percent of songs about breaking up are about being left rather than initiating the end of a relationship.[13]

Conceptions of innate male and female characteristics so often found in Mandopop are remarkably traditional and conservative.[14] Mandopop lyrics portray men as considerate (*titie*), generous (*guangda*), hard-hearted (*xinchangyaoying*), independent (*zili*), tender, gentle, and feminine (*wenrou*), tolerant and forgiving (*baorong*), and vigorous and energetic (*youli*). Women are depicted as following men's lead, placing their own needs as secondary to men's, and as needing to endure hardship (*rennai*). They are also portrayed as being emotional and illogical and are consistently depicted as being dependent (*yilai/yifu*) on men, agreeable and yielding (*roushun*), childish (*haizi qi*), cute (*ke'ai*), gentle, headstrong and capricious (*renxing*), innocent and pure (*danchun*), kind and forgiving (*renci*), meek and frail (*rouruo*), passive (*beidong*), pretty (*piaoliang*), as well as tender, gentle, and feminine (*wenrou*).[15] Notably, these characteristics often contradict each other—women are portrayed as being both headstrong and passive, just as men are depicted as both hard-hearted and tender. This provides a window view to the remarkable flexibility of gender-constructed images in Chinese-speaking Asia.

Mandopop's men are portrayed as doing what they want for their own reasons—they are active, free like the wind (*feng*), and drifting/wandering (*piaobo*). In contrast, women are depicted as being stationary and waiting.[16] Mandopop's pervasive theme of women waiting for men is in part an extension of Taiyupop. In part it depicts the fast pace of Taiwan's urbanization. In 1949 slightly less than 25 percent of Taiwan's population lived in cities with a population of fifty thousand or more.[17] By 1988 approximately 70 percent of Taiwan's population was living in cities of this size.[18] The waiting theme in both Mandopop and Taiyupop was in part a reflection of a male exodus to the cities to find better employment opportunities while women stayed in the villages, raising the children and waiting for the men's return.[19]

It is true that lyrical depictions of women promote remarkably traditional gender roles. It is also true that men show appreciation of songs that support such gender roles. Yet men also identify with the female speakers in such songs. In part this is an extension of a second set of literary traditions dating back to Warring States poetry (480 BC to 221 BC) in which men used female characters in their poems. In such cases male poets frequently used female speakers to symbolize their own emasculated and powerless condition in the face of government injustice. In turn, campus songs drew on this tradition by also using feminine voices to represent the people and men to represent a seemingly unreasonable and often oppressive government.[20] Mandopop draws on these traditions, which reinforce conservative gender roles while simultaneously subverting them in the process of having both men and women identify themselves with the female speaker. These poetic and lyrical traditions cast women in secondary roles, but both women and men identify with them and view women in these mediums as more humane, and indeed more human, than the male/state being critiqued.

Mandopop also consistently portrays women as gentle, tender, passive, and, more often than not, victims to men's caprice. Its persistent portrayal of women as harmless victims is striking in its contrast with images of dangerous hypersexual vixens that appear in women's songs from far more conservative cultures[21] as well as from China's 1930s jazz movement.[22] China's traditional literature and religious imagery was replete with images of female spirits who used their sexual wiles to destroy men, often sucking the life out of them. Chinese religious imagery also depicts women as either dangerously polluting or as all-powerful deities.[23] Given this cultural heritage, the presentation of women's images in contemporary Mandopop is surprisingly sexually restrained and unthreatening.

One explanation for the shift from dangerous vixen to the Madonna complex (the religious figure, not the performer) links to women's greater power as consumers in the modern age. Traditional fiction and religious parables were for the most part written by and for men, whereas Mandopop centers around women's lives, dreams, and frustrations, in large part because women have equal buying power in the music industry.

To the degree that Mandopop is political, this is framed in terms of romantic relationships. Ke Yonghui and Zhang Jinhua point out, for example, that the song "Men's Talk," while overtly describing a woman's frustration that her lover will not speak with her of certain matters that he willingly discusses with his male friends, contains an underlying critique of men's continued attempts to exclude women from certain traditional spheres such as politics or commerce.[24] Yet, although Mandopop lyrics often contain underlying complaints about gender equality, they naturalize gender relations in songs and leave little room to question whether or not there are problems with such dating relationships, marriage, conceptions of women and men, or the patriarchal social structure as a whole.[25]

Because most women's songs are written by men, it is fair to ask whether they represent a female ideal that is being molded by men for male pleasure in a usurpation of women's voices and power.[26] This is not simply male hegemony, however, for songs that misrepresent women's feelings about themselves do not sell, and successful songwriters are few.

Mandopop also gives voice to the hardships that women face rather than the threat that men might feel women represent. The women I interviewed in both Shanghai and Taipei clearly enjoyed Mandopop's depictions of women as angelic martyrs, and the majority of them embraced Mandopop's use of the full range of lyrical adjectives listed above.

The term *wenrou* is another example of the complex gender alignments in these songs. Most commonly translated as "tender," *wenrou* also encompasses nuances of being caring, sensitive, and feminine for women and, for men, quite effeminate by Western standards. To be successful, both male and female Mandopop performers must lyrically and visually perform *wenrou* identities. While this presents traditionalist concerns in the case of *wenrou* women, the *wenrou* male stands for antitraditionalism in portraying vulnerable, non-patriarchal men.[27]

Because Taiwanese lyricists write songs for a wide array of performers, including both women and men from Taiwan, Hong Kong, and the PRC, a singer's persona can be taken into account and exploited to add to the feeling of a particular song. Writing songs to complement each artist's image, which is fundamentally tied into a singer's gender, provides lyricists with a far wider range of expression than if they were to write for one performer alone.

To gain a better sense of the lyrical framing of gendered identities in Mandopop songs, I will now present three songs written by Taiwanese lyricist, performer, and producer Jonathan Lee (Li Zongsheng). Hailed as the prince of love songs,[28] he was one of the first and most important lyricists leading the way in the transition from the campus songs movement of 1977–1981 to Taiwan's contemporary commercial Mandopop.[29]

From the mid-1980s to the mid-1990s Jonathan Lee was without parallel as a Mandopop lyricist, and the people I interviewed in both Shanghai and Taipei repeatedly spoke of him as understanding women's hearts and eloquently writing poetic verse that expressed women's hopes, desires, and frustrations. Indeed, his success was so phenomenal that several people told me that they bought CDs because he had written the songs, without regard to who the performer was—he is the only songwriter to gain this distinction in my interviews. Several examples of his work are provided below.

The first song, "Realization" (Lingwu), is performed by Taiwan's performer Winnie Hsin.

REALIZATION (Lingwu)

[Chorus 2] *Ah! Duome tong de lingwu*	[Chorus 2] Ah! What a painful realization.
Ni ceng shi wo de quanbu.	You were once my everything.
Zhi shi wo hui shou lai shi lu	Only now I look back on the road where I came from

de mei yi bu dou zuo de hao gudu.	and see that each step was so lonely [*gudu*].
Ah! Duome tong de lingwu.	[Chorus 2 continued] Ah! What a painful realization.
Ni cong shi wo de quanbu.	You were once my everything.
Zhi yuan ni zhengtuo qing de jiasuo,	I only hope for you that you can break free of love's shackles,
ai de shufu,	love's constraints,
renyizhuizhu,	follow your own heart,
bie zai wei ai shou ku.	do not suffer again for love.

Here, Winnie Hsin sings about the painful realization that her long-term lover was so selfish when leaving her, concluding with the parting statement to her former lover, "I only wish for you that you can break free of love's shackles, love's constraints, follow your own heart, do not suffer again for love." This is an exceptionally complex song in that through the lyrics sung by this female performer one can almost hear her lover's male voice as she paraphrases his reasons for leaving her. Thus, we have a man writing a song to be performed by a woman, criticizing a man by using his stereotypically male language.

This was the song that brought Winnie Hsin overnight success.[30] Tellingly, it is widely thought that the song's popularity is in part due to the fact that it related to her real-life divorce.[31] The fact that she "naturally" cries when she performs this piece also conveys this sense of authenticity to the audience. The statement that she only came to fully understand herself in her unsuccessful struggle to communicate with a male romantic partner is also a common one in Chinese-language pop music.[32]

Jonathan Lee also wrote the lyrics for this next song, performed by Hong Kong performer Sandy Lam. The song depicts a relationship in which the female protagonist senses that her lover wants to leave her, though he has not broached the subject.

BECAUSE OF YOU I AM BLOWN BY A COLD WIND
(Wei ni wo shou leng feng chui)

Wei ni wo shou leng feng chui	Because of you I am blown by a cold wind.
Jimou shihou liu yanlei.	When I'm lonely the tears run from my eyes.
You ren wen wo shi yu fei.	There are people who ask me if it is true or false.
Shuo shi yu fei?	Speak, is it true or false?
Keshi shei you zhende guanxin shei?	But who really cares about another?

"Because of You I Am Blown by a Cold Wind"[33] conveys a deep sense of despair. At its core is a disillusionment with her lover, whom she thought she could count on. Because of his betrayal, she no longer has faith in others. In keeping with the material I presented in chapter 4, a strong sense of loneliness and isolation is emphasized by the despair and seemingly rhetorical question as to whether anyone really cares. As with the song "Realization," a failing relationship leaves the singer feeling isolated, not only from her estranged lover but from her entire social network. Note the stereotyped "female" passivity and actions (crying, waiting, forgetting) as written by a male lyricist in both of these songs—I will return to this point in a moment.

Elaine, a thirty-year-old graduate student in Taiwan, explains this song:

> In this song her "ex" boyfriend is not really her "ex" because they have not officially broken up. The lyrics are written from a woman's point of view. Men—especially Asian men—can be cowards in relationships they don't want to continue. They don't tell girls that they don't love them anymore. When they want to break up with girls, they just act distantly, and then they wait for the girls to leave on their own.
>
> The girl [in this song] felt that something was wrong with their relationship, and she kept waiting. The first sentence, "Because of you I am blown by a cold wind," indicates that you've been giving me the cold shoulder for a long time and I'm waiting, in the cold wind, for you or your response—until she gets the answer from him. And when she's tired of waiting, she demands an answer, just a simple answer to set her free from the waiting and uncertainty.[. . .]
>
> When the girl finally brought up the question and demanded a definitive answer, she wanted the man to be totally honest about it—not to be afraid to make her sad and try to comfort her—which would result from his sense of guilt. Men feel guilty about initiating the break-ups, that's why they aren't direct.[34]

Elaine expertly links the content of this song to wider cultural mores. In Elaine's view, the song says as much about men as women. She links the poetic allegory of being blown by a cold wind with the man's emotional coldness, and she ties the themes of the song in with what she sees to be prevalent interactions between men and women in relationships. These lyrics therefore successfully capture both the sentiment of heartbreak and a common dynamic in which Taiwanese men emotionally withdraw from relationships rather than directly stating that they want to break up. This, Elaine asserts, links to a failing on the part of many Taiwanese men, who she feels should be more brave and honest in breaking up with women.

The popularity of this song suggests that Elaine is not alone in relating the lyrics to real-life experiences. Her account also supports the views of many of the other people I interviewed, who stressed that Jonathan Lee writes good "women's songs" because he is sensitive to their plight and an able poet who describes their emotional responses to such situations. The way that Elaine effortlessly spins an entire story to fit the poetic framework outlined in the song also highlights the fact that people listening to such songs are active participants in the songs' storytelling rather than purely passive consumers.

Mandopop's emphasis on women's ability to withstand hardship is partially inspired by Buddhist ideals of endurance, forgiveness, and accepting fate.[35] Men's songs also employ Buddhist imagery—for example, the common depiction of men as "tolerant and forgiving" (*baorong*) as noted above. Yet in Mandopop's dreamscape, women are far more forgiving than men and consistently employ passive vocabulary such as "to endure" (*rennai*) and "to depend on" (*yilai*).

Part of the pervasive theme of passive acceptance in Mandopop is related to a common religious motif of attributing the end of a relationship to fate. For example, the Buddhist term *yuanfen* frequently appears in Mandopop songs.[36] *Yuanfen* refers to someone's karmic relationship with someone one has known in another life and is often used to explain the end of a relationship with terms such as "no *yuanfen*" (*wu fen*) or "have *yuan* but no *fen*" (*you yuan wu fen*), meaning that one was destined to meet someone but that the relationship was destined not to work out. Drawing on this religious worldview, Mandopop's women are more likely to lament, and then accept, their fates rather than protesting ill treatment at the hands of men.

In addition to Buddhist themes of forgiveness, one can also find Confucian spheres that relegate women to the home and Taoist/folk religious conceptions in which the world is a balance of opposing forces in which *yin* is female, dark, and passive, and *yang* is male, light, and active. As Chen Qianjun has pointed out for Cantopop, there is a lyrical framework of juxtaposition in Mandopop, with pairings such as "heaven and earth (*di/tian*), mist and water (*wu/shui*), men and women (*nan/nü*), […] to advance and retreat (*jin/tui*), true and false (*shi/fei*), old and new (*jiu/xin*), bright and dark (*qing/an*), and distant and close (*yuan/jin*)."[37] This is an extension of dualism that is embedded in the language. For example "do you want this?" is literally "want no want?" (*yao bu yao*); "is that ok?" is "good not good?" (*hao bu hao*). This linguistic duality helps naturalize conceptions of *yin* and *yang* in which the world is made up of a binary system of different but complementary elements, which is the basis for the most fundamental conceptions of gender in China and Taiwan.

As a point of contrast to the women's songs I have presented above, let us now examine one final example of Jonathan Lee's lyrics, as performed by the internationally renowned Hong Kong action star Jackie Chan.

HOW CAN IT BE? (Zeme hui)

[Chorus 1] *Yankan luoye zai qiufengli fei.*

[Chorus 1] In the glance of an eye a falling leaf floats in the autumn wind.

Na ci neng mei de rang ren xinsui.

It carries itself so beautifully it breaks a person's heart.

Moufei jieju yao xiang zheyang cai dui wuyuanwuhui.

Can it be that in the end it is like this, facing each other without resentment or regret.

Zong you xie wangshi rang ren wuyanwudui.

Some past events render a person speechless.

Aiqing zai xianshili die de fensui.

In reality love crushes (*fensui*) us.

Weihe zai shiqu suoyou yihou haishi bu neng mingbai?

Why, after losing everything can [I] still not understand?

Zeme hui?

How can it be?

As with the previous two songs, "How Can It Be" conveys heartbreak and a certain despair at the speaker's helplessness in the face of a fickle partner. Yet this anger is expressed very differently according to the gender of the singer. In "Because of You I Am Blown by a Cold Wind," anger is expressed through the singer's rejection of new suitors and her condemnation of her friends. She expresses the hope that she can forget, "to put things in the past," "to put it aside." The song "Realization" contains a bitterly sad parody of her ex-lover's language. Her initial yearning for revenge gives way to the singer accepting her fate and stating that she hopes that her lover will get what he wants (though admittedly, with notable passive aggression). In both of these songs there is a certain passive resignation.

In Jackie Chan's song "How Can It Be?" the tone is not one of resignation or limited forgiveness. Instead, the song expresses fiery anger, sung in loud, outraged indignation. The vocabulary speaks of crushing/smashing (*fensui*) and chasing (*zhui*) combined with themes of unbridled passion or anger that is conveyed both by the lyrics and the singing style. In stark contrast with the other songs reviewed here, the male performer does not express an acceptance of fate—nor does he forgive. Such anger and aggressive language can also be found in popular songs such as David Tao's "Black Tangerine" (Heisi liuding) or Chang Cheng Yue's "Let's Break Up" (Fenshou ba), to name a few

This is certainly not the only form of manhood evinced in Mandopop—a point I will explore in greater depth in the next chapter. Indeed, Mandopop makes vulnerable heartbreak, gentleness, and what Western viewers might classify as androgyny a prerequisite for male performers.[38] Yet it does highlight some of the differences in the thematic ranges of songs performed by women and men. Because all three songs presented here were written by the same songwriter, we are witness to the ways Mandopop lyricists mold their songs to match the singers' gendered personas.

Jonathan Lee is the best-known Mandopop lyricist, but he is hardly alone. The lyrical themes in "Realization" and "Because of You I Am Blown by a Cold Wind" are extremely common in women's songs, and these examples only stand out as being more eloquently worded than most.

We have already examined the lyrics for Winnie Hsin's song "Realization." Now let us examine another song she performed that was written by Yao Qian, another exceptionally successful male lyricist from Taiwan.

SCENT (Weidao)

[Chorus 2] *Xiangnian ni de xiao.*	[Chorus 2] I miss your smile.
Xiangnian ni de waitao.	I miss your coat.
Xiangnian ni de bai wazi	I miss your white socks
he ni shen shang de weidao.	and the smell of your body.
Wo xiangnian ni de wen	I miss your kisses
he shouzhi dandan yancao weidao.	and the slight smell of tobacco on your fingers.
Yiyi zhong ceng bei ai de weidao.	Memories of the feeling (*weidao*)[39] of once being loved.
Jintian wanshang de xinshi hen shao.	Tonight's worries are very few.
Bu zhidao zhe yang suan hao bu hao.	I don't know if this is good or bad.
Chiluoluo de jimo chaozhe xintou rao.	This naked loneliness (*jimo*) has left my feelings confused.

In this song, Winnie Hsin sings of her longing for her former lover's scent, ranging from the smell of tobacco on his fingertips to more everyday items such as his white socks. By focusing on the sense of smell, the male lyricist Yao Qian seems to consciously employ a "woman's" perspective in his artistic expression. In part this can be seen as a male construction of female sensibilities, but when I teasingly asked several women if Taiwanese women had a fetish for white socks (as the lyrics might suggest), all of them laughingly protested. Yet after a short pause many of them spoke in more serious tones about the ways that the song's lyrics accurately capture the sense of scent-related nostalgia—relating how comforting the smell of clean laundry was, for example.

Mrs. Chen, a forty-six-year-old Chinese-language teacher in Taipei, suggested that the white socks represented that the singer was dating a married man—

otherwise, she reasoned, his socks would not be clean and white.[40] After I gave a presentation at the National Taiwan University of Arts, a female audience member suggested that white socks represented non-marital domesticity for more or less the same reason.[41] She further suggested that the girlfriend's habit of washing his socks represented the unrealized domestic future they might have had. Elaine, whom I quoted above, said that the fact that the singer even missed her lover's socks simply demonstrated the extent of her love for him.[42] Little Mei, an elementary school teacher just outside of Shanghai, and Little Hong, who works in a department store in Shanghai, had the following to say about the white sock allusion.

> LITTLE MEI: Well, the smell of clean laundry is quite nice, right? The socks
> are white, suggesting they are clean.
> LITTLE HONG: Ya, and you might see something and think of a person—
> maybe a certain kind of clothes. Even white socks might remind you of
> someone, right?[43]

In examining the array of responses to one song we are again confronted with the remarkable flexibility of interpretations and the listener's ability to project his or her own experience onto them. There is a level of consistency in all of these comments, however, in that each of them assumes that women perform domestic services for their lovers. Equally interesting is that all three women categorized domestic service as an act of love. The songs are indeed male creations, then, but they also capture the sentiments of the female audience and reflect broader cultural expectations concerning gender roles.

As a last example of the female performer/male lyricist dynamic, I will present another of Jonathan Lee's songs, performed by Sandy Lam. Unlike the other songs I have presented, this song is portrayed as one woman's advice to another.

SCARS (Shanghen)	
Nüren du you de tianzhen	Only women have the strength
he wenrou de tianfen.	of natural innocence and tenderness (*wenrou*).
Yao liu gei zhen ai ni de ren.	You should save it for someone who really loves you.
Buguan weilai duo ku duo nan	No matter how bitter or difficult things become in the future
you ta pei ni wancheng.	he will be with you completely.

This is an exceptionally complex song in that it is performed by a female and presents itself as one woman's advice to another, though it is written by a man. Thus, statements such as "only women have the strength of natural innocence and tenderness" or "if you love bravely then you should bravely leave him" sound like sisterly advice. Perhaps more importantly, these statements are *taken* as sisterly advice by the listeners I have spoken with—although most listeners are aware that this song was written by a man. Both the female and male audience members are therefore complicit in male constructions of female identity.

When I asked Angel, a twenty-five-year-old marketing executive in Taipei, what she thought about the Mandopop's male lyricist/female performer dynamic, she responded:

> You know, sometimes men behave badly but they know it. That's why they can write songs from a woman's perspective—because they also know right from wrong—they know that they've done something bad so they express it by writing these songs.[44]

As articulated above, Angel, Elaine, and several other women I interviewed believed that male lyricists come to an understanding of women's songs through distinctively male experiences.[45] Such statements stress that men and women are innately different while simultaneously revealing underlying assumptions that gender identity is fluid (men can understand women, men can express "women's" feelings, etc.). These assertions emphasize that songs such as this are thought to reflect real, rather than purely imagined, experiences—both for the performers and for themselves. The fact that the people I interviewed linked this with actual male and female behavior in Taiwan also highlights this point. Male lyricists create gendered stories, therefore, but they are tales that female listeners readily recognize as their own.

Image Maintenance: Visual Presentations of Women in China and Taiwan

Women have long been representational symbols in China, from associating Republican Era women's spending habits with the strength of the nation,[46] to the occupational prowess of Cultural Revolution's Iron Girls,[47] to concerns that women's sexuality could endanger the health of the race.[48] It is therefore no surprise that the image of what a woman should be has changed as rapidly and dramatically as the nation itself.

The 1930s Shanghai jazz era portrayed women as independent, charming, full of energy, and overtly sexually alluring.[49] Beginning with the PRC's inception in 1949, the centrality of musical and visual imagery of women as erotic objects in Shanghai's Republican Era gave way to the lyrical loss of individuality as "productive female masses" who sacrificed themselves for the good of the party.[50] Two decades of "gender erasure" followed, in which equality of the sexes largely meant that women were expected to look and act like men.[51] In turn, the sole musical styles in the first two decades of the PRC was a loud, marching-band style, or booming, politically focused opera that created a musically masculine ethos that Nimrod Baranovitch has described as "lacking in *yin* and abundant in *yang*."[52]

Beginning with the Taiwanese performer Teresa Teng and continuing with modern-day Mandopop stars, Gang-Tai pop offers images of women, both lyrically and visually, that seem to embody all of the attributes that the PRC had discouraged in the previous decades. The performers, while not exactly flaunting their wealth, were clearly well off economically and sported the latest haircuts and clothing styles from their own countries as well as from the United States and Japan. Indeed, by the 1990s, the mix of Western and Chinese fashion and cosmetics inspired by China's new market economy created a look so alien to the earlier visual images in the PRC that they might have been taken directly from a Japanese or Taiwanese photo shoot.[53] While many Western scholars view women's fashion with a good deal of ambivalence, for contemporary Chinese women, lipstick and mascara, high heels, and skirts have become signs of liberation from patriarchal state control.[54]

In my interviews in both Shanghai and Taipei, women and men described female Mandopop stars as having some combination of the following attributes: *wenrou*, cute (*ke'ai*), and sexy (*xinggan*). There is also the "spicy/hot girl" (*lamei*) image which describes a more overtly sexual appearance, though it is still quite restrained in dress and mannerisms compared to an American pop star. These varied images are essential components of the ideal Mandopop star, and, by extension, young women in both China and Taiwan.[55] In addition to Mandopop lyrics, the visual presentation of female pop stars creates contrasting images of women as they mediate between their modern setting and traditional ideals for female personhood.

Although this has been shifting in the past few years, most Taiwanese female singers present themselves as attractive yet conservative-looking personas. In contrast, foreign-born or foreign-dwelling female singers of Chinese ethnicity have far more freedom in this regard. For example, Karen Mok from Hong Kong and Coco Lee (who was also born in Hong Kong but raised in the United States and made her musical career while living in Taiwan)[56] have more leeway to wear sexier clothing and to move in more provocative ways than native-born Taiwanese singers in both performances and their music videos.

Similarly, in the 1990s, A-mei, a Taiwanese aboriginal performer, was also able to present herself as a more sexual persona than ethnically Chinese performers—drawing on Taiwan's fetishized conceptions of aborigines who are thought to be more sexual and better singers. The leeway given to these artists is acceptable to

Figure 9. *Lamei* (spicy/hot girl) Taiwanese performer Jolin Tsai poses in front of her own photo. She is so popular that her pictures can be seen in shop windows on virtually any main street in Taipei or Shanghai. Photo courtesy of the *Taipei Times*.

a Taiwanese audience because they are, by virtue of their Chinese identities, "one of us," while they can also fill the role of sexualized other.

A telling account is when I showed Miss Li, Miss Yang, and Mr. Zhang, whom I cited above, a picture of the performer Jolin Tsai. They all agreed that she was very sexy in the picture. A long pause ensued after which Miss Li said, "She looks aboriginal, doesn't she?"[57] Everyone enthusiastically agreed. In the course of the interview it became clear that all three of them were aware that Jolin is not a Taiwanese aborigine, but in aligning her as "looking like" an aborigine they maintained Taiwanese images of self as more pure and civilized in relation to the hypersexualized images of ethnic others.[58]

In the beginning of her career, A-mei used these stereotypes to her advantage, wearing clothing that was far more suggestive than most Taiwanese could get away with at the time. Her garb reinforced stereotypes of ethnic otherness—for example, when she wore leopard-skin miniskirts or grass tops with her midriff exposed.

Figure 10. Taiwanese Mando-pop star Elva Hsiao promoting the Hong Kong movie *Infernal Affairs*. Note that she transforms stereotypically masculine attire into a very feminine look. Photo courtesy of the *Taipei Times*.

Yet Taiwan has never had leopards, and few of her outfits are authentic traditional aboriginal garb. Thus, A-mei's "nativeness" becomes so generalized to be meaningless outside of a performative context. In keeping with Taiwan's attempts to distinguish itself from the PRC, A-mei, as an aboriginal performer, is often taken as the symbol of Taiwanese identity both by Taiwanese and the PRC government, as demonstrated when President Chen Shui-bian selected A-mei to sing the Taiwanese national anthem at his 2000 inauguration, as well as with the resulting PRC ban of her performances.[59] By the same principle, Hong Kong and Taiwan performers, by virtue of their peripheral regional associations, have more leeway than PRC performers in much the same way that the PRC allows ethnic minorities to express more sexualized persona that confirm self-aggrandizing images of the Han majority.[60]

A second part of the female repertoire is a cute (*ke'ai*) look. This is widely thought to be a direct import from Japan, which is in turn exported to the PRC. Though the desirability of cuteness is fading in Japan,[61] Taiwan still embraces it with a fervor. Rainie Yang, the darling of Taiwan's commercials, is Taiwan's foremost representative of the *ke'ai* image and is said to be attractive because she looks young and innocent. Michelle (Mixue) and Vicky (Weiqi) of the group Kissy (Qinjin)[62] also surround themselves with images of childlike fantasy. In their advertisements and album covers they are depicted in various playful poses with bubbles and cute, rounded Chinese characters and English letters. At other times they pose with lollipops or a jump rope, or cartoon hearts are drawn into their picture. Yet on closer inspection, Michelle and Vicky's clothes are neither purely childlike nor innocent in that they are far more revealing than would be acceptable for a child in China or Taiwan. The cute look demonstrates a prevalent fetishization of youth in Taiwan that can also be seen in cinema, television, and daily life. Many believe this to be a cultural import from Japan that is in turn exported from Taiwan to the

Figure 11. "Cute Sexy": Taiwan performers Michelle and Vickie from the group Kissy (Mixue Weiqi) presenting a fantasy world of eternal innocence while simultaneously posing as objects of sexual desire.

PRC. As with the lyrical models that I have already presented, PRC pop stars have also gone through a dramatic transformation of visual self-presentation, from Mao-suit-clad patriotism to Taiwan's *wenrou* style.

It should be noted that there is often a remarkably thin line between performers' images of *lamei* and *ke'ai*. Jolin Tsai might appear to be young and cute to many Westerners, but her figure, jewelry, dance moves, and general self-presentation place her firmly in the category of *lamei*. Indeed, Jolin consciously transformed her image from cute and innocent to *lamei* in 2002. When she returned to the music scene after being out of the spotlight for a year, she had lost weight, dyed her hair reddish brown, wore more revealing clothing, and re-emerged with more sophisticated dance moves.[63]

Although *wenrou*, *lamei*, and *ke'ai* (or some combination of the three) are the most prevalent forms of femininity portrayed in the Gang-Tai pop industry, three Hong Kong–based performers in particular have added a new rebellious component to the mix: Karen Mok, Anita Mui,[64] and Faye Wong.[65] Widely seen to have more independent and unruly characters, they provide an important counterpart to the *wenrou* persona that most Taiwan and Hong Kong female performers present.

In truth, however, there is often a remarkably thin line between these categories, and it is quite possible for one star to represent more than one of these images at the same time. Indeed, some of the most successful female performers—Anita Mui, Faye Wong, and in more recent years Jolin Tsai, for example—are successful precisely because they (hip-)hop so agilely from roles of feminine *wenrou* to *lamei* and back again.

Conclusion

Harris Friedberg asks the important question of popular culture: "Does it, in the debased coinage of politics, trickle down or bubble up?"[66] The answer is inevitably both, in that pop culture simultaneously creates and reflects audience concerns. The gendered roles I have just reviewed for modern Mandopop draw on traditional conceptions of women and men, including cultural values stemming from Buddhism and ancient conceptions of *yin* and *yang*. The theme of women waiting while men roam, a modern-day extension of traditional Confucian separate spheres, is also extremely prevalent in these songs.

One of the more fascinating aspects of audience reception of Mandopop is that the constructed nature of the gendered identities performed with the songs seems to be willfully overlooked by most of the people who listen to the music. Mandopop lyricists gain fame in their own right, and audiences seem as familiar with who wrote a particular melody and set of lyrics as with the performers themselves. The degree to which audiences willingly embrace a song written by a man as a "woman's song" forcefully demonstrates that it would therefore be a mistake to conceptualize Mandopop as a unilateral, top-down power hierarchy, but rather, in a very Foucaultian sense, it is a matrix of often contradictory cultural forces.

Women's roles are defined in such songs by a cultural emphasis for women to endure hardships rather than overcome them. Thus, women become allied with traditional values of perseverance and the acceptance of suffering. By emphasizing women's virtues and men's shortcomings, women's Mandopop can be seen as a critique of both men *and* modernity. This is perhaps surprising considering that the modern age has ostensibly been more beneficial to women in Taiwan and the PRC's urban elite—granting the right to divorce, work, and travel, for example. Yet in many ways these women have also borne the brunt of today's more uncertain world—there is far less predictability concerning their partner's intentions concerning marriage, for example, and as such their personal and economic lives are less stable.

Susan Napier, in explaining the central role of women in Japanese anime, points out that "it is so often the female subject who most clearly emblemizes the dizzying changes occurring in modern society."[67] Eric Thompson, writing on Malaysia, notes that women, especially, are faced with conflicting notions of gendered identity in the modern age in that Malaysian women must mediate between traditional Muslim and modern global standards of beauty, modesty, and fashion.[68] Similarly, contested domains can clearly be seen in both lyrics and in female Mandopop stars' presentation of selves. Far from going for shock value or challenging established norms, in many ways Mandopop lyrics are more conservative than the real world.[69] Yet given the hyperpolitical histories of both the PRC and Taiwan, Mandopop's apolitical stance becomes an intensely radical statement. Its celebration of the individual becomes both a personal choice and an ideology for what China's future should be. The lyrical, visual, and performative conceptions of women associated with Mandopop thereby become models of thought and behavior for Chinese youth who are anxious to leave the past behind but uncertain of what road to take for the future.

Mandopop paradoxically reifies notions of innate differences between women and men while simultaneously undermining these very same images by allowing men to express these emotions by singing or listening to songs (or writing them), as well as by encouraging women to perform men's favorite tear jerkers. Mandopop songs are strongly gender coded by both lyrics and performances, yet because audiences are fully aware that men write many of the songs that women sing, the songs are also a testament to a faded line between women and men.

Shifting from the individual to state identities, we see equally perplexing paradoxes. As I noted in the introduction of this book, Taiwan is extremely vulnerable in the face of the PRC's economic and political might, yet it shapes PRC thought and behavior to a startling degree and clearly dictates PRC trends ranging from fashion and makeup to music, KTV, and conceptions of relationships and womanhood. Feminine-coded ideals thereby win out over masculine rhetoric, and the feminine is associated with modernity and a desired identity of globalized participation in world culture. Thus, Mandopop revolves on several axes—female/male, subject/ruler, Gang-Tai/PRC—and in each case *yin* seems to be victorious over *yang* as a way to humanize the masculinist rhetoric of state politics.

Importantly, the common playing ground here is on what would normally be thought of as female thought and behavior. Taiwan pop's retaking of the mainland is therefore a gendered invasion. The conservative lyrics assert women's secondary positions, yet this paradoxically allows the feminine values to supplant masculine hegemony. Mandopop's embrace of traditional gender roles thereby creates a feminized modernity that contrasts "male"-oriented spheres such as politics or economics with "female" realms of emotion in a framework that leaves little doubt as to women's virtues and men's failings. Mandopop's new gender values supplant masculinist national discourse, which is stigmatized as being bound to an unpleasant period in history—as well as uncouth. This is inevitably contrasted with its feminine counterpart, which stands for transnational participation and cosmopolitan sophistication. In this cultural setting—so rife with contradictions—in spite of continued cultural preferencing of men, women have become the cultural ideal for what the majority of Chinese hope to be.

CHAPTER 6

A Man for All Occasions

Charisma and Differing Masculinity in Mandopop

She remembered thinking that he had come out of nowhere, survivor of some early trauma she could only begin to imagine, and that the waves he gave off when he sang were his attempt to soften the memory of that time. But she didn't believe that any more; Hashi's hell wasn't behind him, it was still there inside him, like a malignant growth, and he sang to get this torment out of him, to spread it around, so as to retain some sort of balance.

—Haruki Murakami, *Coin Locker Babies*

The young people no longer observe the rights. They no longer know to respect chiefs and elders. Only through wailing and tears can we recall the grandeur of our past.

—Paiwan aborigine female from *Sounds of Love and Sorrow*

An essential component of the Mandopop industry's bid for success is the degree to which it can create viable images of ideal women and men with love songs that audiences can relate to. The previous chapter addressed constructions of women's identities in such songs and the ways in which Taiwan's pop has helped to redefine femininity as paradoxically both more traditional in its personality schema and more modern in its transnationalism. As I noted in chapter 2, though women's roles are shifting toward the Taiwan model, masculine identities have become a far more contested domain in the PRC. In part this is because Mandopop's female identities are returning to traditional Chinese conceptions of women as passive and emotional sufferers, which does not pose a threat to patriarchal traditions in the ways that androgynous men might. In part this is also a tension between conflicting images of hypermasculinity in Hong Kong action films and the relative androgyny of Mandopop.

The *Wenrou* Male—Tender Androgyny in Mandopop

Wenrou, a term most often translated into English as "tender," denotes characteristics of being caring, sensitive, and, when describing men, fairly androgynous. This version of effeminate masculinity has none of the stigma that it might carry in the United States. Instead, the *wenrou* male is seen as an ideal in Taiwan, and in many ways it is a far more common version of manhood than other models among the middle and upper class.[1] Taiwanese men are often contrasted with Chinese men in the PRC (by people from the PRC, Taiwan, and the United States) as being more gentle (*wenrou*) and feminine (*nüxing hua*) than their mainland counterparts. This perception is in part created by the Mandopop industry, but it is also a pre-existing notion that contributes to the success of Taiwan's Mandopop.

Susan Bordo's study of American men who go to gyms to sculpt their bodies into symbolically powerful phalluses[2] reminds us that Americans have quite a—if you will pardon the double entendre—*rigid* idea of male physiques and personas. In using this analysis as a comparative point for Taiwan, one sees that Americans are "reading" the texts of Mandopop according to artificially naturalized conceptions of idealized masculine and feminine roles in the United States. Indeed, many people in Taiwan joke that, with the exception of anomalous Westerners, if you go to a gym all of the men with tattoos are hoodlums (*liumang*) and all of the men without tattoos are gay. This is of course an exaggeration, but it does highlight the fact that unlike in the United States, where androgyny is often looked down on as lacking manliness, in Taiwan muscular bodies are often associated with stigmatized lower class occupations, gangsters, male gay culture, or barbaric Western physiques.[3]

Wenrou male Mandopop stars' images also allow for a wider range of emotional expression than the relatively constrained roles available to heterosexual men in the United States. This assists in packaging melancholy, loneliness, and emotional vulnerability for the female audience, and in providing an ideal for caring men who make up for the men in women's real-life relationships.[4] Because it also creates a set of images for the male audience to identify with, Mandopop stars create ideals that women and men read slightly differently according to their needs.

Several scholars have commented on androgyny as a desirable trait in Western pop music as well. Simon Frith has suggested that homoerotic admiration of boyish bands is an essential component of Western pop.[5] Sheryl Garratt asserts that women are drawn to androgynous male performers in pop more than to macho rockers precisely because of their feminine attributes. In other words, she quips, "androgyny is what they want: men they can dress like and identify with, as well as drool over."[6]

In the previous chapter I presented the active and somewhat violent imagery in the lyrics of Jackie Chan's song "How Can It Be?" in contrast with the passive vocabulary in the women's songs that I was examining. Notably, even in Jackie Chan's song there is a marked sense of vulnerability that undermines the otherwise macho persona portrayed in the song. Even more importantly, this is but one form of masculine expression in such songs. As a point of contrast, let us now examine Richie Jen's song "A Heart That Is Too Soft" (Xin tai ruan), which Mrs. Lu, whose interview I provided in the previous chapter, mentioned as a typically "male" song.

A HEART THAT IS TOO SOFT (Xin tai ruan)

Ni zongshi xin tai ruan,	Your heart has always been too soft,
xin tai ruan.	a heart that is too soft.
Duzi yi ge ren liulei dao tianliang.	All alone, by yourself crying until daybreak.
Ni wuyuanwuhui de aizhe nei ge ren.	You don't resent and don't regret that you loved that person.
Wo zhidao ni genben mei name jianqiang.	I know you are fundamentally not that strong.

The content of this song is reminiscent of "Scars" (see chapter 5) in that both songs advise a female friend to be strong and break up with her undeserving lover because her relationship is causing her to suffer needlessly. Yet, the gender of the performer dramatically affects the feeling of each song. "A Heart That Is Too Soft" is sung with a sprightly melody—evoking a feeling that the male singer is trying to cheer the woman up. In contrast, "Scars" is sung in a sorrowful tone, and one gains a sense of shared suffering and understanding from both the sound of the performer's voice and the melody. Thus, the performer's gender creates very different feelings of "you women are this way" and "we women are this way," though both are written by men.

I found the lyrics to this song on the Web, but the person who had posted them used the male form of both "you" (*ni*) and "he" (*ta*)—a common written mistake in less professional settings. The result was that I was unsure if the song was about a woman being left by a man, or a man being left by a woman—or, far less likely given Taiwan's mainstream views on homosexuality, about a man being left by a man.

Yuanyuan is a twenty-eight-year-old user interface designer for a computer software company in Taipei. Her name is a homonym for "round, round," which her friends often tease her about. Because she is extremely petite, the name suits her in much the same way that the name Little John fits the towering character in *Robin Hood*. When I asked Yuanyuan about the gender of the people in this song, she scanned the lyrics and immediately said:

He is singing and giving advice to a female friend. The song is definitely about a woman—see, she has a "soft heart"—and she is waiting for him. Women always wait in these songs. But you are right, it is a little confusing that they don't write the feminine version of "you." Also, the song is sort of androgynous [*zhong xing*] so you can't be absolutely certain it is about a woman—a man or a woman could sing this song and a man or a woman could relate to these experiences.

[Moskowitz:] That's funny, because another woman I interviewed specifically mentioned this song as a quintessentially male song.

[She laughs] That probably has more to do with the singer than the lyrics. [The performer] Richie Jen is very much the typical image of the *wenrou* male, so the woman you interviewed was probably thinking of the singer rather than the song itself.[7]

Figure 12. Wu Bai introduced the cool image to Taiwan's musical scene.

Yuanyuan's account is interesting on several levels. First, she instantly labeled the song as being about a woman because of the term "soft heart," linking the lyrics with prevalent conceptions of innate female characteristics. Her assertion that it is an androgynous song markedly differs from Mrs. Lu, who thought of it as a prime example of a distinctively male song, forcefully demonstrating the flexibility of such texts.[8] Also, note the use of *wenrou* to describe androgyny. Importantly, this "androgynous male" is used to represent what she sees to be a quintessential image of manliness.

Vivian, a twenty-one-year-old stewardess in Taipei, and I had the following conversation concerning which artists were *wenrou*.

> VIVIAN: The term *wenrou* is usually used with women, but if a guy is considerate (*titie*) we might describe him as *wenrou*. I don't know if I'd say Richie Jen was *wenrou* though—usually this term is used for people who are more androgynous (*zhong xing*) such as Zhang Fei, who is a popular personality on a television show.
> MOSKOWITZ: What about David Tao?
> VIVIAN: David Tao is not *wenrou* but some of his songs are.
> MOSKOWITZ: And Jay?
> VIVIAN: No, I don't think so.
> MOSKOWITZ: What about Wu Bai?
> VIVIAN: [Laughs] No way! [Laughs again]
> MOSKOWITZ: What about Leslie Cheung?
> VIVIAN: Definitely! When Leslie Cheung was alive he was THE *wenrou* performer.[9]

Vivian's responses evince the wide range of degrees associated with the term *wenrou*. On one end of the spectrum is Taiwanese rock star Wu Bai, for whom Vivian finds the very association with *wenrou* to be laughable. On the other end of the spectrum is Leslie Cheung, whom she takes to be the epitome of *wenrou*. Somewhere in the middle of these two extremes is Vivian's assertion that David Tao is not *wenrou* though some of his songs are. I will now provide three of David Tao's songs to explore this point further.

The first song, "Black Tangerine" (Heisi de liuding), is a hard rock melody.

BLACK TANGERINE (Heisi de liuding)

Jintian wo xinqing you yidian guai guai de,	Today I'm in a strange mood,
keshi shuo bu lai daodi weisheme.	but I can't say why this is.
Hao xiang you yi xie beishang de zhengzhao,	It seems as if there are some
	symptoms[10] of sorrow,

keshi bingyin bu zhidao.	but I don't know the disease.
Tou shang you juse de jiazhou yanguang,	The orange California sun shines on my head,
wo de koudai zhi you heisi de lauding.	[but] my pocket just has black tangerines.
Wo zhi you yi ge lanse de ganjue,	I just feel blue,
bu yao wen wo weisheme.	don't ask me why.

The melody of "Black Tangerine" is reminiscent of hard-edged U.S. alternative music. The setting also self-consciously aligns the song with David Tao's Los Angeles roots, as does his use of English words.

In chapter 3 I addressed the issue of the prevalent use of English key words in Mandopop songs. Admittedly, sometimes the English makes for odd combinations, such as the song's line "*jiushi qing ni* leave me alone" (so please just leave me alone) which not only uses English and Chinese words in the same sentence but also employs English syntax with Chinese vocabulary. Yet, as I argued in chapter 3, within the context of Chinese and Taiwanese cultures this kind of innovation makes sense—and the music is, after all, presented to a Chinese-speaking audience.

New concepts accompany English language vocabulary. Simple statements such as "I feel blue" (*Wo you lansi de ganjue*) in Chinese have new and interesting nuances in a country where one does not use this phrase to denote a feeling of melancholy. Instead, many people in Taiwan take it as an interesting turn of phrase with no specific meaning. Rather than being a Western imitation, therefore, the lyrics, as in so many Mandopop songs, are a successful blend of East and West. I find it unlikely, for example, that a Western alternative song would wax poetic about the autumn falling leaves with heavy metal guitar in the background as this song does.

Manhood is also an essential component of the song. Note the decidedly male theme (within the context of such songs and Chinese culture) of being unable to express his emotions. The lyrics repeatedly describe his desire to cry, which could be read as feminine, but the melody alternates between a soft melancholy tone and loud hard rock. This, combined with images such as moldy fruit, feeling like a little worm, and other general nastiness not often found in women's songs, mitigates the possible *wenrou* in this instance.

I will now provide two additional songs from the same CD as "Black Tangerine" that highlight David Tao's *wenrou* repertoire. Unlike the hard electric guitar of "Black Tangerine," this song employs soft instrumentals, and Tao's voice ranges from alto to soprano.

ANGEL

Yi ge ren (yi ge ren)	One person (one person)
zai renhai piao.	floating in a sea of people.
Shuohua de ren zhao bu dao.	[I] can't find someone I can communicate with.
Shei gei wo wenrou (yongbao wo)	Who can give me *wenrou* (embrace me)
yongbao dang wo ganjue xin kuai	and embrace me until my heart feels like
yao suile?	it will break?

In this song David Tao expresses some of the same sentiments as in "Black Tangerine"—self-loathing, loneliness, isolation, and an inability to properly convey his feelings are all present in both songs. Yet whereas the first song is loud and angry, in this song he is the epitome of *wenrou*—focusing on images of holding hands, embracing, and relying on the woman's strength because he is so emotionally vulnerable.

"Lullaby," from the same CD, presents a second dimension of *wenrou*, shifting the focus from romance to parenthood.

LULLABY (*Yaolanqu*)
(Vocals and a piano only)

Kanzhi	When I look
ni wuxie de lian.	at your cherubic face.
Zhe shijie hai xiang ge leyuan.	This world still seems like a paradise.
Haizi,	Child,
mengli xiao de tian.	smile sweetly in your dreams.
Ai wo huai li ni keyi anmian.	In my bosom you can sleep peacefully
Yingzi	A shadow
shi konglong wanju.	becomes a dinosaur toy.
Ni de xiangxiang zai ezuoju.	Your imagination plays tricks with you.
Yueguang zai qiang shang he	You play with the moonlight on the wall
ni wan youxi.	like a toy.

Wawa's contributions to David Tao's songs were the only examples I found of a woman's creation of male Mandopop performers' lyrical expression. It is therefore impossible to use these songs to generalize women's construction of male identity in the way one could with men's construction of women's identities. David Tao does not have children, but Wawa does. One might assume, therefore, that Wawa is at least partially responsible for the Chinese poetic images (such as the leaves falling in autumn) as well as quite feminine vocabulary and imagery such as holding a child to one's bosom. What the songs do offer is a powerful example of the flexibility of Mandopop men's images from macho to maudlin *wenrou*.

Even male performers' choices of English names are often in relationship to their *wenrou* images in that they often choose names that end in "ie" because it is thought to sound more diminutive. A few examples from artists mentioned in this chapter are Leslie Cheung, Richie Jen, and Jackie Chan, who straddles between the image of his masculine martial arts and his more "cute" disarming humor.

Humor and Masculinity

As became evident in the previous section of this chapter, lyrically men can, and indeed must, have a wide range of expression—from overtly masculine to *wenrou*. In the previous chapter I presented Jonathan Lee's lyrics to examine the ways in which he creates one discourse in women's songs and a more active and angry imagery for male martial artist Jackie Chan's song. Jonathan Lee, in writing "I Have Something to Say" (below) for himself to perform, displays a combination of the two. He is passive and soft-spoken in contrast to his father, who shouts him into temporary silence. Within the context of these songs, the lyrics convey a very masculine resistance and hostility to an authority figure, yet the song emphasizes his status as a *wenrou* male when he seeks emotional communication, as opposed to his more masculine father, who is stereotypically unable to show his love.

The song opens with the sound of a loudspeaker announcing that one of the students is in trouble. Jonathan Lee repeats the melody, singing "la la la" with a soft melancholy that belies the repeated statement that he is singing a happy song.

I HAVE SOMETHING TO SAY (Wo you hua yao shuo)

Yexu ni faxian wo	Maybe you have discovered that I
nianqing de yan zhong muguang shanshuo.	have youthful rose-colored glasses.[11]
Ni shifou kanchu wo	Do you see me
wei qiantu youlu mihuo?	perplexed and worried about the future?
Ni bu neng zhi shi shuo shi waimian de shijie rang	You cannot just say that it is the outside world that
ni shen qing lengmo.	has made you emotionally cold and detached.
Weihe bu kaojin wo?	Why can't you be closer to me?
Ni ke zhi wo xinli xiang sheme.	Then you could understand what I was thinking in my heart.
Shei nenggou bu fan cuo	Who can grow up without making mistakes
chenzhang de lu ni ye cuo zuo guo.	along the way.

You xie hua bu zhidao ying bu yinggai dui ni shuo.	There are some things that I don't know if I should say to you.

Ni Shuo, "Huh? Ni zai xiang sheme?!	You say, "huh? What are you thinking?!
Ni zuo le cuo!	You did it wrong!
Cuole zai cuo!	Wrong and wrong again!"
Ni shuo "Huh?	You say, "Huh?
Ni zai xiang sheme?!	What were you thinking?!
You sheme hua hao shuo?!	What do you have to say for yourself?!
Ni shuo!	Speak!
Weisheme bu shuo?!"	Why don't you speak?!"

This song is both a cry of joy and a song of sorrow. Lyrically, it is a tragic depiction of a man unable to communicate with his emotionally distant father and the anger and heartbreak this causes the son. Yet although the lyrics are quite serious, its presentation is extremely humorous. The first time one hears the father's voice, he shouts, rather than sings, the lyrics. The second time the father belts out the lyrics with a chorus of baritone singers with operatic flair. The song begins and ends with the sound of a cash register opening and closing to set the rhythm of the song and to accentuate the father's obsession with commerce. Thus, the listener laughs in spite of the song's serious subject matter.

Other Mandopop songs are more straightforwardly humorous, such as Jonathan Lee's song "Seventeen-Year-Old Girl's *Wenrou*" (Shiqi sui nüsheng de wenrou), a satire in which he waxes poetic about how a seventeen-year-old girl's *wenrou* is "really like, you know" (*qishi shi hen neigede*), mocking young women's vacuousness in much the same way that "valley girls" have become an object of satire in the United States. A female chorus sings in exaggeratedly girlish tones in the background and creates an overall effect of a song from the American movie *Rocky Horror Picture Show*.[12] He goes on to sing about how he admires "her bright heart and dim eyes" and her "simple heart and complicated expressions" and ponders on whether or not she spends every day waiting for her graduation ceremony. He then sings, "But then, I'm only guessing. / I'm not a woman / and I haven't been seventeen for quite a long time now."

David Tao's song "My Anata" is a parody of *enka* with mixed *enka* and alternative melodies, using Japanese key words and sung with an exaggeratedly pitiful voice. In the song he wonders if Anata is leaving him because he hasn't had any news from her in two years and three months. He begs her to tell him what he has done wrong because "I never hit you back and I never screamed back at you [. . .] I diet for you and I get drunk for you."

Chang Cheng Yue's more irreverent songs are inappropriate to print here because of their graphic sexuality, but I will cite a few of the more innocuous examples. The song "Think Too Much" (Xiang tai duo) is about his crush on a woman who has a part-time job at McDonald's. Because he doesn't have the courage to actually talk to her, he expresses the desire to eat eight hamburgers a day so that he can spend more time there, and he fantasizes about getting a part-time job at McDonald's so he could work with her. In his song "Male and Female Dog" (Gou nan nü)—slang for adultery—he sings about a woman he likes so much that he thinks of her every day and uses his pillow to "represent her." He sings, "My pimples / are still not gone / and everyone tells me I have really bad breath. / Maybe that's why / she doesn't like me."[13]

Humor seems to be in the domain of male songs to the point that no one I spoke with could provide an example of humor in a woman's song. Mr. Zhang, whom I quoted in the previous chapter, mentioned humor as a primary reason for his preference for "male songs."

> Chang Cheng Yue also has a lot of songs about being heartbroken, but his songs are not sad. He laughs at himself about it, that's why I like him.[14]

Humor crosses different masculine identities, ranging from the *wenrou* Jonathan Lee to the hypermasculine lyrics of Chang Cheng Yue. When I asked Chang Cheng Yue why humor seemed to be so rigidly contained within the male sphere, he replied:

> I think Eastern culture is still sexist (*da nan ren zhuyi*). This is changing. For example you hear people say "girl power"[15] so men and women are becoming more equal. But Eastern culture is still influenced by these traditional concepts. We've made progress but it is still difficult.
>
> Now within this concept it seems pretty obvious that men can still get away with more than women. So if a woman does something like that, people will say "Huh? How can she do something like that?" So with regards to men using humor in their songs more than women I think it basically boils down to this. If a woman does the same thing men will say "that woman is not respectful enough, or she is not circumspect (*jiandian*) enough." It is because of traditional Eastern thought. So a woman can't be completely free in her expression.[16]

In addition to Chang Cheng Yue's insights on the need for women to act more demurely in Taiwanese culture, I suspect that humor also falls in the male domain as an extension of the traditional value of intellectual prowess. This draws on, and reinforces, the dichotomy of men as associated with culture (the arts, education, medical achievement, and science) and women with nature (childbirth, physical beauty, etc.). Sherry Ortner has demonstrated that these are not in fact logical constructs—yet as she points out, they do persist throughout much of the world.[17]

Becky, a thirty-year-old assistant at a law firm and part-time performer in Taipei,[18] demonstrates the ways in which gender boundaries are naturalized in Taiwan:

> Men are more creative. They don't talk much so they write to express themselves. Women talk more so they can express themselves through conversation.[19]

Becky's assertion that men are more creative than women is not very flattering to women—a point that is particularly striking since, in addition to playing covers of other performers' well-known hits, she writes the lyrics for her own songs. On the other hand, she also claims that men are more constrained in emotional expression, which suggests a worldview in which women and men have their own set of strengths and weaknesses.

The fact that the humor in such songs is also often self-belittling (such as Mr. Zhang notes for Chang Cheng Yue in the above quote) is also significant, for the songs emphasize the performers' masculinity through the demonstration of intellectual prowess, while simultaneously reducing the potential threat of male Mandopop stars' patriarchal authority. Therefore, self-belittling humor allows the listener to identify more closely with the star.

A second gendered component is that the songs are often challenging authority figures or norms, which would conflict with female Mandopop stars' presentation of themselves as "good girls." Humor thereby creates a distinctively male sphere in Mandopop without overtly claiming to do so.

This self-belittling humor is part of a larger Mandopop ethos of maintaining an image as an average person. Hiroshi Aoyagi suggests for Japan, for example, that unlike Western stars the Japanese music industry consciously promotes an image of Japanese idols being more like the girl or boy next door, which the Japanese refer to as "life-sized."[20] It is tempting to apply this analysis to Mandopop as well since most stars are good singers but not great, and cute but not stunning. Yet the category of "life-sized" appears to be an American construct—or rather a construct that was taken from Japanese discourse and erroneously applied to Mandopop.

Whether looking at musical talent (Bobby Chen, Jay Chou, Qi Yu, Stefanie Sun, and Wu Bai readily come to mind) or physical attributes (Elva Hsiao and Jolin Tsai are absolute ideals for physical beauty—they are certainly not thought to look like the girl next door), idols are not perceived to be "average." Rather, there is the normal tradeoff, as in any musical genre in this visually mass-mediated industry, between musical talent and physical attractiveness. I therefore suggest that this demonstrates an element of "life-sized" without the term encompassing stars' entire identities.

Visual Masculinities

The interplay between the music and movie industries is a large part of many male and female performers' images. Mandopop stars (especially from Hong Kong) almost always become movie stars, and in turn actors will almost equally inevitably enter the music industry. They also appear in advertisements, game shows, and television dramas.

The masculine images of individual performers such as Wu Bai overlap between their musical identities and the violent action movies they act in. Cinematic presentation also reinforces the *wenrou* male personas such as the roles that performers such as Leslie Cheung play.

Bobby Chen offers a third form of manhood in that he is seen as neither hypermasculine nor *wenrou*. That he is not easily categorized in this way fits his

Figure 13. Jay Chou, who played a macho swordsman in the movie *Curse of the Golden Flower*, is portrayed here as *wenrou* on a postcard that came with the CD *November's Chopin*.

songs, which break the KTV relationship (see chapter 1) of other songs both in their atonality and wider thematic range. Instead, like Jonathan Lee, his status is that of a poet of Taiwan's modern age.

Hong Kong performer Andy Lau has two distinctive identities. On screen, he often plays macho roles such as policemen, gangsters, or, in the case of the movie *Infernal Affairs*,[21] both at the same time. In contrast, in his Cantopop and Mandopop roles he often presents a *wenrou* persona. Similarly, Jay Chou is best known for his sophisticated melodies, but he is also associated with his lyrical critiques of society and for his somewhat adolescent male images on his CDs and music videos—including dressing himself up as a ninja and rescuing, and then threatening, a girl dressed in a high-school uniform. His role in the movie *Curse of the Golden Flower*[22] was one of a hypermasculine martial artist. Yet many of Jay's songs are also sung in a soft, tearful voice that demonstrates a relative ease in switching from macho to *wenrou* roles. In the postcards that came with his CD *November's Chopin* he is dressed in frilly shirts that highlight his *wenrou* side. Mandopop men therefore become what Jeroen de Kloet has called "intertextual chameleons"[23] that hop from one persona to the next according to the medium. As such, they have a wider range of expression than many female performers.

Conclusion

Given Western biases, it is hardly surprising that the androgynous image of pop is often compared unfavorably to masculine rock in Western press and academic discourse. Yet this should be challenged. With characteristic insight, Richard Dyer emphasizes that disco, for example, though often discounted by scholars, offers a welcome alternative to phallocentric macho rock,[24] introducing a romanticism denied in that genre.[25] Androgynous Mandopop male roles should not be seen as a shortcoming, therefore, but as something that enriches the musical sphere through offering new alternative masculine voices in both music and culture.

If, as I have argued, Mandopop men have a wider range of gender roles to select from than women, they are still constrained by expectations that they not appear too feminine. The greatest limitation placed on men in this regard can be found in the prevalent motifs that they need to be strong and that they have a difficult time expressing their feelings. This draws on gender stereotypes that women are considered to be emotional and men to be rational. Though in many ways women are stigmatized by this stereotype, it can also be seen as empowering to women in that they are portrayed as having more emotional depth than men.[26]

The flexible images of Mandopop stars suggests a range of culturally acceptable gender roles. Indeed, the degree to which these roles overlap is as noteworthy as when they fall into distinctly male or female categories. As I have suggested in the previous pages, the *wenrou* male should not be seen as lacking masculinity in the context of Mandopop, but rather as possessing characteristics that all men would have if real men could only be so perfect.

CHAPTER 7

Mandopop Under Siege

Culturally Bound Criticisms of Taiwan's Pop Music

[Jay Chou] saw them come and go, pretty boys who could barely carry a tune, divas who had the attitude but not the talent, boy bands whose members were chosen for their dance steps instead of their voice chops.
> —Kate Drake, *Time Asia*

These highly commoditized performers are young, good-looking, stylish, and usually possess little or no talent at all.
> —Leo Ching, "Imaginings in the Empires of the Sun: Japanese Mass Culture in Asia"

But pop is not *only* [emphasis his] a dream machine: perhaps, like witchcraft in another age, it is the unofficial chronicle of its times, a history of desires existing in the margins of official history, which, except at rare moments of rupture, do not speak but act. In setting out a history of today, popular culture etches the contours of a history of tomorrow in that it "feels" a social atmosphere in its earliest, unformulated stages.
> —Antoine Hennion, "The Production of Success: An Anti-Musicology of the Pop Song"

In the following pages I will examine the cultural biases embedded in critiques of Mandopop. In the 1980s and early 1990s, Taiwan's popular music swept across China. Many in the PRC government reacted to the values embedded in Taiwan's lyrics with mistrust and disdain, expressing a fear that Taiwan and Hong Kong's cultural incursion would result in the PRC's loss of national identity. On the other side of the strait, people in Taiwan complained of Mandopop's fast pace and changing nature and linked this to similar trends in Taiwan's society. More recently, several of Taiwan's scholars have critiqued Mandopop for promoting patriarchal gender roles, and English-language publications complain of a lack of individualism in that songs are produced in teams of composers, lyricists, and performers. In the following pages I will examine the cultural contexts of these critiques in order to come to a better understanding of what is, after all, the most popular Chinese-language music in the world.

Critiques from the PRC, Taiwan, and in English-Language Publications

As noted in chapter 2, the 1980s were a time of intense liberalization in the PRC, resulting in an opening to mass-mediated culture from Taiwan and Hong Kong. Taiwan's Mandopop was at the forefront of the PRC's introduction to the outside world, but the wild enthusiasm for this music caused a backlash among many in the PRC government. Several Western scholars have documented the PRC government's extremely hostile reaction to Mandopop produced in Taiwan and Hong Kong, which said it was "too loud and too vulgar," "morally decadent and aesthetically empty," and going so far as to label the music as pornography. As an extension of this, the PRC government called for the nation to fight against Gang-Tai pop's "evil influences," representing it as an emasculated "illness that was inherited from the 1930s" and labeling it as "spiritual pollution" and "the sounds of a subjugated nation."[1] In the 1980s, people in the PRC could be arrested simply for listening to Gang-Tai pop that had not been authorized by the state.[2]

An examination of PRC musicologist Leng Sui-jin's writing provides us with a representative sample of the PRC rhetoric on Mandopop from that era. Although on the whole fairly positive about the value of Gang-Tai pop, Leng warns of a dangerous subset of this genre, labeled as "obscene and pornographic songs":

The lyrics are full of sexual incitements and dissolute and licentious interests. [...] The use of strong rhythms and "slippery" sounds enforces the effects of frivolity and sexual arousement [sic]. Moral decline, a life sunk in drunkenness and dreams, and hysterical behavior are all shown through the use of great wave-like trills of reeds and throaty musings of saxophones.[3]

The PRC critiques that I outlined above are strikingly culturally bound. Their condemnation of pop as pornography, for example, arose in an authoritarian state that, as Kay Ann Johnson and Judith Stacey have pointed out, had long acted as patriarch to its subjects.[4] Thus, the concern lies not with the quality of the music, per se, but with a perceived danger of disrupting a communist utopian ideal.

Perhaps surprisingly, Beijing rock musicians share the PRC government's anxiety that Gang-Tai pop will usher in commercialized values and an ensuing loss of national identity, disparaging Gang-Tai pop as inauthentically "Chinese."[5] Similarly, a blog written by a PRC music critic goes as far as to compare Taiwanese musicians with prostitutes, saying that they only go to China to make a quick buck and concluding with the question, "but when they leave with their money, what is left for us"?[6] The critic continues by stating that China's music industry has unquestioningly followed Taiwan's musical trends, resulting in losing its own sense of identity, and likens Taiwan's musical influence on China as an act that "counter-invades the mainland."[7] Thus, the Chinese elite's dismissal of Gang-Tai pop is part of a larger resentment of popular culture from Taiwan, Hong Kong, and the United States for ushering in crass commercialism and Western decadence.[8]

One can find similar worries concerning the loss of national identity in Taiwan's scholarship. Liang Hongbin, for example, uses Mandopop as an emblem to express a fear that Taiwan is losing its cultural identity because it has absorbed so many influences from countries such as Japan, Korea, and the United States.[9] Another common complaint is linked to the temporal nature of popular music. Taiwan musicologist Liu Xing, for example, in comparing Japanese-era Chinese-language popular songs to Mandopop in the 1980s, laments, "Why are yesterday's popular songs so much better than today's?"[10] He asserts that earlier genres had a charming simplicity in contrast to modern Taiwan pop, in which "the tempos are very fast, they are performed fast, they are sung fast, and they are quickly forgotten."[11] Liu links the speed of the music with the pace of society and at times compares the growing complexity of society with his own development, complaining that his growing sophistication as a musicologist has ruined his appreciation for song.[12] Somewhat predictably, Liu links the pace of change in both music and society with "foreign influences."[13]

Although Taiwan's elderly are more likely to make such statements, I have spoken with several younger people who shared these views. Xiangyu, a twenty-six-year-old graduate student in Taiwan, points out that such nostalgia is connected with Taiwan's tremendously rapid economic development and urbanization.

> People listen to songs from a period to remember that time. Some people always think of the future, many prefer to think back to the past. Taiwan is very small but very complicated, so we like to listen to music from a simpler time.[14]

These statements are representative of a common ethos of nostalgia among many in Taiwan. For Taiwanese, nostalgia, an already problematic concept, is even more of a quandary, for in romanticizing their past they idealize a time when Taiwan

was a colony of Japan or later, for all intents and purposes, of the KMT. This inter-
pretive retelling of history is therefore yet another example of an invention of tradition[15] or a nostalgia for a past that never existed.[16]

In Taiwan's more recent scholarship there have also been several critiques
about the effect of Mandopop's conservative gender roles and patriarchal themes
on youth.[17] If this analysis seems more familiar to a Western reader than the PRC
rhetoric outlined above, it is because of the dramatic influence that Western political and academic developments have had on Taiwan's growing feminist movement. This scholarship also reflects many Western academics' assumptions that
good music should be ideological, even revolutionary in nature.[18] In this sense,
Western critiques bear a remarkable similarity to the PRC state's disdain for the
incorrect political messages of such songs.

Contemporary English-language publications describing Mandopop are also
extremely culturally bound. Although they do not express concern with the pernicious degenerate effects of pop, they quickly dismiss it with the implicit critique
that it does not live up to the authors' Western expectations of what the music
should be. Surprisingly, this is often voiced in the popular press that is ostensibly
promoting the industry, such as an English-language Taiwanese newspaper article
that states, "[T-Ho Brothers' (Tiehu Xiongdi)] sound is the first of its kind to be
born in Taiwan, where pop music is largely a pantheon of pretty faces."[19]

Similarly, a *Times Asia* article covering Jay Chou, the undisputed king of Mandopop from 2002 to 2008, spends most of the article with the somewhat unexpected sales angle that he is unattractive, which, the article implies, adds to his
legitimacy as an artist. The article also notes that unlike other pop stars, Jay began
his career writing music for others and therefore possesses talent, rather than the
external packaging, that it asserts is the norm for Mandopop:

> Male Canto- and Mando-pop stars are supposed to be born with connec-
> tions, grow up with money and emerge in adolescence lithe, androgynous
> pinups, prefabricated and machine-tooled for one-hit wonderdom and, if
> they're lucky, lucrative B-movie careers and shampoo commercials. How
> did a kid with an overbite, aquiline nose and receding chin displace the
> Nicholases and Andys and Jackys to become Asia's hottest pop star?
> The explanations starts somewhere back in that stuffy studio, with the
> discipline and the songs and the revolutionary idea that the music actually
> mattered.[20]

To the degree that Taiwan pop is addressed at all in Western scholarship, it is often
also quickly dismissed. Leo Ching, for example, has this to say about Mandopop
stars:

These young "idols" [. . .] are usually given a particular character trait—cute, naïve, rebellious, or animated—most of which are completely different from their personalities. These performers almost never make or play their own music; their songs are written and produced by a professional songwriter.[21]

This is not to denigrate Leo Ching, for indeed I think he is one of the best scholars working on Taiwan. But that is exactly what is troubling about this. What does it mean when one of the most notable scholars of popular culture in Taiwan so casually dismisses an entire genre of mass-mediated production? Although English-speaking scholars have been fairly careful about putting such views into print, flippant or condemnatory statements about the music can frequently be heard in conferences, colloquia, and casual conversations among academics—including scholars that specialize in ethnomusicology of Taiwan.

Even when Western academics do not dismiss Taiwan's pop quite so readily, their analysis has its own set of cultural biases. The book *Music at the Margins: Popular Music and Global Cultural Diversity*,[22] for example, while not overtly hostile to Taiwan's music, also reveals an underlying ethnocentrism. The authors correctly attempt to problematize the idea of Western cultural domination as a one-way flow "from the West to the rest."[23] Yet if their stated goal is to undermine concepts of Western hegemony, the underlying logic is that the worth of music lies in the degree to which it enters the Western market.

Second, they assume that what Taiwan has to offer is an integration of traditional Chinese sounds and instrumentation, thereby attempting to force Taiwan into the position of representing a Chinese minority through its association with traditional "ethnic" music. The result is a study replete with statements that support Western hegemony and ignore Taiwan's accomplishments:

Canada, the Netherlands, and Taiwan do not have strong contemporary popular music forms of their own in comparison with India, Jamaica, and Nigeria, although Taiwan's Chinese musical tradition offers the possibility of adding highly innovative traditional elements to the world's popular music pool.[24]

As Allen Chun and Ned Rossiter have emphasized, the conception of "world music" is in fact a European and American reinforcement of perceived transnational hierarchies.[25] Leaving aside the fact that Taiwan is combined with such disparate nations in this blanket statement, the authors fail to ask the Taiwanese what *they* think about their own music. Thus, Robinson and her coauthors unquestioningly judge Taiwan's music according to their own standards of what qualifies as excellence and what does not.

Robinson goes on to state that "Taiwan, as a former colony of Japan and a long-time enemy of mainland China, has been more concerned about cultural encroachment than cultural encouragement.[26] As I have already noted, music produced in Taiwan is exceptionally popular in Hong Kong, the PRC, and any region with a sizeable Chinese-speaking population (Malaysia, Singapore, and Los Angeles readily come to mind). The fact that Taiwan is one of the centers of music for one of the largest populations of the world is ignored here, and the West is exalted as setting the standard for musical success.

These English-language critiques of Mandopop are ultimately based on a perceived failure to live up to Western standards for the genre. I have spoken with many Westerners in Taiwan who support their condemnation of Mandopop by pointing out that performers do not usually write their own songs. Such statements demonstrate a rather unquestioning belief in the superiority of individualism. Several scholars have warned that one should be wary of teleological views of Western modernity and emphasize that other countries have other modernities.[27] Mandopop, as an enduring if always shifting marker of modernity, should also be given its own space as an alternate cultural/musical form.

It is true that in the case of Mandopop, a singer's styles overtly rely on what Irene Yang has called a "singer-composer relationship"[28] rather than the image of an individual creator/performer such as those found in some U.S. pop. As Theo Chou, an American-born Chinese who mixes music for record companies in Taiwan points out, this does result in Taiwan's music companies having more say in a song's production than in the United States.

> I think in terms of what you want on an album [music companies] are more relaxed about it in the U.S. This is because the majority of artists in the United States now are singer/songwriters. Because they write their own songs and they are putting their own stuff on the album it's harder for the music company to say no.[29]

Taiwan's method of musical production is not necessarily a worse system than the one used in the West. It may also point to a greater rationality that prioritizes the end product more than binding the music to individual star's identities. In theory, if one could take the very best songwriter and team him or her up with the best singer and composer, one would get a better result. In other words, why not coproduce songs if one can combine the best of each person's skills? Mandopop's acceptance of coproduced songs may also point to a greater focus on teamwork rather than the obsession with individual performance. This, in turn, reflects on larger cultural conceptions concerning the superiority of group effort over individualism.

Indeed, unlike in the United States, Mandopop lyricists and composers also become famous in their own right. Xiangyu, the Taiwanese graduate student quoted above, said:

> Chen Xiaojuan wrote the song for Karen Mok's [Mou Wenwei] CD "[i]" which won so many awards. Chen Xiaojuan's boyfriend is a famous producer. Another producer stole her boyfriend's heart so she wrote this song "Love" (Ai).[30] There was a lot of public outcry about her winning because Karen Mok can't sing well, but the songs are so good she won the Golden Melody Award for best singer. In the news and web pages there was lots of really heated discussion about this. People, even if they can't sing well, get the "best singer" award. Shouldn't it mean she is the best singer?[31]

Such remarks highlight the public personas of songwriters in Taiwan. In a sense Xiangyu's statements support the critiques that performers are empty shells. Yet on another level it also points to the public's high expectations for every member of the song's creation and performance team.

Lyricists write songs with certain singers in mind and sell their songs to the performer whose public persona best fits the mood of what they have written. The following account is from an interview with Michelle, a twenty-four-year-old lyricist from Taipei.

> I've been working for this company for about a year now. I had been writing songs for myself—whether or not I'm going to be the one performing them. But my boss told me I have to start writing songs for others—professional songwriters have to write songs for others, after all.
>
> I have to know the performer's personality, what fits best for her. I listen to their songs for inspiration as to their personality and I will meet them for coffee to talk with them to get to know them, and I explore what they have done already and then I write songs for them. But it's not like I just want to do what they've done before. I put new energy into the songs, so it is a blend of their and my styles really.[32]

So yes, these songs are constructed, but perhaps less arbitrarily and more creatively than it might at first seem. Note Michelle's statement at the end of the above quote, for example, in which she stresses that she wants to leave her own mark on the music she composes rather than just doing what the artist has done before. Because songwriters and performers are mixed and matched, Mandopop performers can explore a wide range of identities, which adds to the complexity of the music.

The Western critique that many Mandopop stars do not write their own songs uncritically accepts conceptions of Western Enlightenment individualism as the only virtuous path. It has been argued that in Japan individualism has more to do with being fashionable or sophisticated than with being independent thinkers.[33] I would suggest that this statement is true in Taiwan as well, and in the West for that matter. Thus, unreflexively accepting the team-produced images of Western pop as individualistic while condemning what is arguably a more honest approach of coproduction in Taiwan says more about Western conceptions of self than about the music. To critique Mandopop with the implication that Western pop is somehow different in these regards ignores all of the people who are part of the production and marketing team for pop music in Western music industries.

Indeed, Westerners tend to lose sight of the somewhat arbitrary nature of what we think of as "natural" guidelines for musical creativity. As Howard Becker points out, there is a cultural consensus in the West that rock and roll should be written by the performer, whereas composers of classical music may also perform but it is not expected that they do so.[34] Similarly, Edward Kealy's examination of the importance of people who do song mixing for the finished product leaves little doubt as to the innately collaborative nature of music production in the West.[35]

The above mentioned English-language commentators on Mandopop embrace the individualistic imagery of Western musical production while losing sight of the constructed nature of such imagery. In doing so, they forget that their cultural standards for creative production draw arbitrary lines that become naturalized over time. Why, for example, do they insist that the songs be written by the performer though they do not care if the music videos are produced by others? Backup bands and sound mixers define a large part of the sound of any given song, even with hits that are "written" by performers. In the 1950s it was understood that performers ranging from Patsy Cline to Aretha Franklin to Frank Sinatra had others write songs for them. In the 1960s, performers such as the Grateful Dead and Jimi Hendrix produced covers of Bob Dylan songs, which became some of their most famous hits. In recent years, the United States especially has been moving toward remakes of both movies and songs.

The truth is that all genres of today's music, ranging from rock and roll to punk to pop to country-western, take songs from other genres and "localize" them to expose their own audience to new forms of song and to demonstrate what their musical genre can do with other musical forms. This is a form of tribute to the original song makers and an important form of creative expression. It also forces the listener to reconceptualize too rigidly defined views of musical genres.

The power of European and American music is in its blending of a richly diverse set of musical traditions from Africa, Europe, and South America, among others. In much the same way, Taiwan's adoption and adaptation of other countries' music should be seen as a vibrant celebration of many different musical traditions including traditional Chinese music and religious performances, as well as American, European, Japanese, Korean, Latin American, Taiwanese aboriginal, and other musical influences.

Another failure of English-language condemnation of Mandopop is that it implicitly refers to "boy-toy bands" and ignores the majority of individual performers, some of whom are quite talented. If we were to do the same for Western popular music, would we really be conveying a sense of the genre as a whole? There is incredible diversity among Taiwan's performers, ranging from Qi Yu's astounding vocal range, to Bobby Chen's somewhat atonal but beautifully poetic songs, to Wu Bai's soft metal grit, to Jay Chou's sophisticated, jazz-influenced R&B. By lumping all Mandopop in one category, English-language critiques reify the image of the Asian other as nameless, faceless clones.

Mass Production, Standardization, and Lyrical Poetry

The condemnation of Mandopop draws on a history of academic dismissal of pop music in the West, which includes the works of Theodor Adorno,[36] Walter Benjamin,[37] and Jürgen Habermas.[38] They seemed to find mass production, and indeed popular culture as a whole, so distasteful that it takes on a vaguely immoral nuance in their theoretical frameworks. Though such ideas are dismissed by most today, the basic assumption that music of resistance is "good" and that standardized music is "bad" can still be seen in later works.[39]

Here too, it would seem, statements on the quality of music is often less about the music itself than introducing the biases of those who have the authority to assess its value.[40] Part of academia's hostility to disco, for example, is in its unabashedly capitalistic image tied in with extravagant expenditures on performances and musical production.[41] Yet rock is also intensely professionalized despite the image it must maintain to retain legitimacy[42]—as opposed to pop, in which, in the words of Jeroen de Kloet, "authenticity is just another style."[43] Dyer also stresses that assumptions concerning disco's innate hegemonic values are problematic in that capitalism's main goal is profit and as such the music industry quite willingly presents social critique as long as it sells.[44] He thus takes to task the notion that music produced within capitalism innately supports the hegemony of its controllers.[45] Citing gay cultural uses of disco as an example, Dyer also highlights the often contradictory messages in the music and the multiple ways in which it can be appropriated by different groups.[46]

In examining critiques of pop music in the West, we see insightful analysis of the commodification of musical genres, ranging from punk to rock and roll.[47] Much of this academic discourse shares the assumption that music's value is in its antihegemonic struggle against society. As Richard Dyer also points out, one should be wary of taking political themes as the only value of pop music.[48]

It is true that Mandopop does have several standardized guidelines. Most songs are about heartbreak. Many of the popular singers are what might be defined in the West as androgynous men or women who, though more sexualized in the past few years, present relatively sexually restrained images in comparison with their hypersexualized U.S. counterparts. Many of these songs include the occasional English word or phrase and are heavily influenced by U.S. melodic styles. Most have simple melodies that avoid syncopation or too wide a vocal range—making it easier for the songs to be sung in KTV. Most songs include themes of loneliness and isolation.

Mandopop is hardly alone in having thematic and tonal boundaries, however. Any genre (blues, classical, and, yes, pop) has a set of melodic structures and lyrical themes—that is what makes it a genre, after all. It is important to remember that there is tremendous variation and innovation within mass-mediated frameworks. As Simon Frith points out, even standardization is a conceptual category that shifts according to the one setting the standards:

> More generally, we could say that such "formula criticism" tends to be genre-centric: minor variations in teeny-bop music (the fact that the stars have different vocal registers, say) are taken to be quite insignificant; minor variations in rural blues guitar phrasings are taken to be of great aesthetic importance.[49]

To the degree that Mandopop does have certain recurring themes, one should also note that from the perspective of the lyricist, here lies the challenge. Not unlike traditional Chinese or English poetry in which one must follow a limited set of rhyming patterns, the Mandopop lyricist must take set themes, and to some degree a fixed vocabulary, and make them fresh, new, and moving. The result can be the tedium one experiences when one examines many Western pop lyrics, but when Taiwan pop gets it right, the results are nothing less than fantastic.

In looking at Western popular literature, John Cawelti argues that all stories are a mix of convention, in which one knows what to expect, and innovation, which makes the story new and interesting—a tradition dating back to Homer and Shakespeare.[50] John Fiske makes an equally important point that Madonna's music and videos are interesting precisely because they draw on previous images.[51] As an example he cites the music video "Material Girl" as a playful reference to Marilyn Monroe in the movie *Gentlemen Prefer Blondes*, which in turn draws on cultural images of blondes in general.[52] Thus, as Andrew Gooden points out, "pop has plundered its archives with truly postmodern relish, in an orgy of pastiche."[53]

Since I began working on this project, the response of most Westerners I have spoken with who are familiar with Mandopop,[54] from professors to businessmen, language teachers, and students, could be summed up with a statement to the effect of "That's a great project, but you have to admit, the music sucks." For the most part, such comments come from Westerners who do not speak Chinese and/ or have not paid attention to the lyrics, which most fans agree are the strength of Mandopop songs. In choosing their favorite songs, most Chinese-speaking audiences focus far more on the lyrics than on melodies.[55] To prioritize the melodies of such songs is therefore an additional Western bias.

In China and Taiwan there is a split in that most people prefer to listen to Western pop when clubbing because of the lively melodies. When at home or in KTV, however, there is a clear preference for Mandopop. A large contributing factor to this auditory separation of spheres is that modern Mandopop inherits a tradition, dating back at least to the 1930s birth of Chinese-language pop music, of adopting poetry as lyrics for its songs. As I noted in chapter 1, an equally important factor that shifts the focus to the lyrics is KTV, which has changed the criteria of many listeners from whether or not one enjoys listening to the music to whether or not it is easy to sing. As a result, with a few exceptions, Mandopop melodies are often relatively simple, avoiding syncopation or erratic stress on particular words. To make a rough comparison with music familiar to the Western reader, the songs of Ray Charles, Bob Dylan, Elton John, and Willie Nelson have fairly simple melodies and the charm of their music is often in the lyrics. As with Mandopop, this is not to say that their melodies are not appealing, but that in ignoring the lyrics one misses the best part of these songs.

Part of the Western perception that Mandopop all sounds the same is because the foreign audience is confronted with it as outsiders. To the uninitiated, country-western, pop, rock, or classical music might seem equally standardized, though fans of each genre would no doubt take offense at this statement. Studies of Western pop culture have pointed out that negative assessments of various forms of pop culture ranging from heavy metal to soap operas are often based on the views of incompetent readers who lack sufficient knowledge to make the genre meaningful.[56] In other words, uninitiated audiences lack the necessary background to appreciate, or indeed comprehend, the nuances of the story being unfolded before them.[57]

Leo Ching points out that scholarship on Japan's cultural influence on Taiwan has both ignored the voices of Taiwanese consumers and wrongly considered them to be passive receptacles to popular culture.[58] In talking with people in Shanghai and Taipei, it becomes clear that there is more to the music than meets the ear. Miss Cai, a twenty-four-year-old college student in Taipei, told me:

> [Mandopop is] more subtle [than songs in the United States]. Taiwan's songs have more imagination. They aren't like U.S. songs which are so direct—U.S. songs have no subtlety.[59]

Miss Luo, a twenty-four-year-old interior designer in Taipei, said:

> I listen to Taiwan pop but I don't really like U.S. pop—it's not that I hate it or anything, I just don't end up buying it. Foreign music is better for clubs. But if I go to KTV I always listen to Taiwan's pop because it is easier to sing in Chinese.[60]

Miss Li, a twenty-eight-year-old nurse in Shanghai, said:

> Americans always hate our music, but I think they just don't understand it, you know? It's like poetry, you can't just glance at it and get it. You really have to savor it for a while to really feel what the song is about.[61]

George Trivino, the music producer I quoted earlier in this book, had this to say about the differences between music produced in Taiwan and the United States.

> TRIVINO: I think the most basic difference is Taiwan's music draws on a lot of different sounds. For example, if you ask about Chang Cheng Yue's CD and what kind of music he does, it is difficult to say because it is not just one genre. He has some songs that sound like hip-hop and some like rock, and some that take elements from both in the same song. But in the U.S. if someone is a rock star he just plays rock, if he is a hip-hop artist he just plays hip-hop. Chang Cheng Yue's albums are a great example of this. Even in one song there are elements from many different kinds of music. The genre is not as important in Taiwan; the music is very hybrid (*hen baorong*).
> MOSKOWITZ: Why is that?
> TRIVINO: Because Taiwan's culture is also very hybrid (*hen baorong*). It includes Japanese influences, Western influences, and native Taiwanese (*bentu*). You know, Taiwan has around twenty-three million people, many of whom are from very different backgrounds and very different places. This is a very unique place. I think that except for the U.S., Taiwan is one of the most hybrid places in the world.[62]

These are just a few examples of statements by people I interviewed who felt that Mandopop was superior to U.S. pop in a variety of ways. To review, Miss Cai emphasized that Mandopop was more "subtle" and more imaginative than Western pop. Miss Luo appreciated Mandopop for more practical reasons—highlighting the fact that it was easier for her to sing than Western music. George Trivino pointed out that Mandopop is less rigid in its musical categorization, which leads to a wider range of musical expression, which in turn draws on Taiwan's extremely diverse foreign and local influences. Keeping in mind that most of the people I interviewed were familiar with musical genres in China, Taiwan, and the West, one might suggest that it is we, not they, who "don't get it."

Importantly, not all songs fit into the stereotypical KTV genre. As a few examples of the creative ingenuity that can be found in Mandopop, David Tao's song "This Evening's News" (Jintian wanjian xinwen) employs no musical instruments. Instead it is made up entirely of the sounds of different people on Taiwan's televised news over a four-day period. Stefanie Sun's song "To Be Continued" (Wei wancheng) begins with the sound of manual typewriter keys being struck to a particular rhythm. This is followed by the sound of the return carriage bell adding to the rhythm, which is then carried out and built on with other instruments. Jay Chou uses a ping-pong ball to set a truly impressive jazz-like rhythm for the background of his song "Third Grade, Class Two" (San nian er ban). His song "Terraced Field" (Titian) is also a sophisticated blend of disparate elements. The background chorus is sung with aboriginal lyrics and melodies. He also sings in Mandarin Chinese using a baritone voice to represent an aboriginal farmer whose pronunciation of "di" rather than "de"[63] marks the different accents of the speakers. As a third element, he uses Mandarin Chinese rap (sung in alto) to represent his critique of society. He employs syncopation (a rarity in Mandopop) to introduce a jazz element throughout the song. These are but a few examples of the ways in which Mandopop integrates the sounds of daily life to create sophisticated melodies in very innovative ways.

Conclusion—Mandopop as Resistance?

On the surface, Mandopop can hardly be seen to be a form of protest—after all, its very name "Mandarin Chinese *popular* music" emphasizes the fact that it embodies mainstream, rather than alternative, ideals. Yet, as outlined above, there is something about the genre that seems to offend just about everybody. From this one must deduce that the music is challenging a wide range of social values.

As is the case with other kinds of transnational pop, there is always the question of whether we are witnessing cultural imperialism or, as more recent studies have shown, an active appropriation and transformation of Western influences.[64]

A model of the cultural appropriation and assimilation of foreign symbols is intrinsically more interesting—and more accurate—than a mythically totalizing force from the West. Yet I also want to avoid the idea that if it is one (cultural appropriation) it cannot be the other (cultural imperialism). As Clifford Geertz has suggested, in making one's theories too neat, one loses sight of the complexities of real life.[65]

Mandopop's sophistication has been overlooked by both lay people and scholars alike. As has become clear in the previous pages, scholars and the popular press in the PRC, Taiwan, and the West critique Mandopop for not living up to their standards of what they think the music should be rather than examining the full range of the music's cultural significance. Although I have defended Mandopop on its own terms, in a sense the question of whether the music is "good" or not is irrelevant. The most important question here, and one that is far too infrequently asked, is why the music is so revered by the largest population in the world. In this framework the question is not, therefore, "why are they getting it wrong" but, rather, what are we missing here?

Given the hyperpolitical past of both the PRC and Taiwan, to be apolitical is a highly political stance. Mandopop embraces modern urban and Westernized lifestyles—yet at the same moment the emphasis on loneliness and heartbreak in these songs expresses individual dissatisfaction with the uncertain world that the artists and fans find themselves in. In a sense, then, as with other musical forms, pop music can be seen as "packaged dissent."[66]

As I have demonstrated in the previous pages, Mandopop has dramatically reshaped PRC culture to make it look, act, and sound more like Taiwan. It has ushered in a wealth of cultural values ranging from new gender roles to reinventions of both traditional and modern aesthetics, thoughts, and modes of behavior. It has introduced transnational and global values in spite of the government's best efforts to prevent this and it has provided a model to prioritize the individual in opposition to state and Confucian ideals.

In allowing people to give voice to their lives in very personal and emotional terms, this seemingly benign music overcomes the almost irresistible forces of both contemporary state demands and traditional Chinese expectations of stoic silence and group orientation. In this sense, these songs of sorrow represent an equally strong impulse to cry for joy—a tearful reminder of the beauty in people's everyday lives and the importance of each broken heart in an increasingly rationalized world.

Notes

Preface and Acknowledgments

1. See Said 1978.
2. Ewen 1984, 4.
3. Adams 1986, vi.

Chapter 1: The Tail Wags the Dog

1. Wells 1997, 206.
2. Y. Shih 2004, iii; Taiwan's Executive Yuan CPC 2006, 2; J. Wong 2003, 153; X. Xu 2002, 323. Taiwan's domestic music market shares these preferences in that Mandopop from Taiwan represents an average of 75 to 80 percent of Taiwan's music market, whereas Western popular and classical music in Taiwan accounts for only 15 to 20 percent (Wells 1997, 208; Iwabuchi 1998, 25).
3. Gold 1993, 911, 917.
4. L. Li 1993, 118.
5. M. Yang 1997, 293.
6. Gold 1993, 910.
7. Futuro Tsai's documentary on Ami aboriginal hip-hop (2005), for example, forcefully demonstrates the extent to which Mandopop has entered into the Taiwanese Ami aboriginal tribe's lifestyles ranging from the incorporation of the music into traditional dance, weddings, and daily life events.
8. de Kloet 2003, 25.
9. See Baranovitch 2003, 208; D. Ceng 1999, 36; L. Li 1993, 20.
10. Baranovitch 2003, 229; de Kloet 2000, 247; de Kloet 2005c, 323; L. Li 1993.
11. Brace 1991, 47–48.
12. Fung and Curtin 2002.
13. Fung and Curtin 2002, 267.
14. Fung and Curtin 2002, 277.
15. Fung and Curtin 2002, 275.
16. See Wells 1997, 207; V. Wong 1998a. Each of these companies has between seven and thirty-three subsidiary labels. For example, in 1998 Rock Records had thirty-three

subsidiary companies, Sony BMG had thirty-nine, PolyGram had forty, EMI had eleven, Warner Music had seven, and Universal had four (H. Lin 1989, 65).

17. NT$162 million. H. Ceng 1997, 35. A mere five years later, in 1971, this number had risen to eight times that amount with an impressive US$39.4 million (NT$1.34 billion) (H. Ceng 1997, 35). Taiwan's music industry continued to thrive, seeing a steady increase from 30.1 million CD sales with a gross profit of US$169 million (NT$5.7 billion) in 1991 to 47.6 million CD sales with a gross profit of US$363 million (NT$12.3 billion) in 1997 (Z. Zhou 1997, 22).

As few points of contrast, Hong Kong's Cantopop generated HK$485 million (US$69 million) in 1992 (Q. Chen 1997, 29). In 1995 Hong Kong's entire musical production (Mandopop and Cantopop, imports and exports) was HK$550 million (US$78.6 million) by midyear (Q. Chen 1997, 29). In 1998 Japanese pop sold US$8.1 million in CDs in Taiwan (V. Wong 1999). In 1994 Hong Kong- and Taiwan-produced Mandopop made up 44 percent of Singapore's music market, accounting for US$86 million in sales that year (Liew 2003, 223).

18. *Asia Weekly* 2001, 47. Victor Wong estimates that Taiwan's 1998 music market totaled US$400 million (V. Wong 1998a).

19. *Asia Weekly* 2001, 47–48.

20. Similarly, Jeroen de Kloet has suggested that the PRC rock movement was born to piracy in that people in China were first exposed to Western rock when buying CDs that had been discarded in the West (de Kloet 2005b, 609). Beijing Rock star Cui Jian, for example, stated that his access to illegal recordings significantly contributed to his education and development as a rock musician (Efird 2001, 69). These CDs were usually cut slightly on the outside rim to make them unsellable, but because CD players actually start from the inside and work their way out, all but the last song on such a CD was still playable, thus making it very marketable in mid-1990s China, which was starved for exposure to foreign music (de Kloet 2005b, 616–617).

21. In 1997, Taiwan produced 476 million CDs, generating US$363 million (X. Xu 2002, 325). From 1998 through 2000 it generated gross annual profits of slightly under US$300 million (*Asia Weekly* 2001, 47; Z. Zhou 1997, 22). In 2001 Taiwan only produced 186 million CDs, generating US$157 million in sales (X. Xu 2002, 325)—less than half of what it had made four years earlier.

Hong Kong was no exception. In 1998 Hong Kong passed new legislation against piracy and within three months police raids resulted in the confiscation of 13.5 million pirated CDs, which was presumably only a small fraction of the total pirated goods (V. Wong 1998c). Japan has also suffered because of piracy but less because of free downloads than inexpensive CD rental shops and sharing among friends (Condry 2006, 190–196).

22. *Asia Weekly* 2001, 47.

23. NT$3.2 billion. For more on plummeting sales in the Mandopop industry, see H. Lin 1989, 140–144; Y. Shih 2004, 52, 91.

24. Taiwan's Executive Yuan CPC 2006, 3.

25. S. Chang 2007a, 11.

26. Two thousand yuan.

27. By one account, this represented 30 to 40 percent of Sony Records' Mandopop revenue in 2002 (Y. Shih 2004, 97).

28. S. Chang 2007a, 13; S. Chang 2007c, 27.

29. George Trivino, interview, March 9, 2006, Taipei.

30. S. Chang 2007b, 35.

31. One billion yuan.

32. Baranovitch 2003, 46.

33. White 1998.

34. Burpee and Mooney 1997; Wells 1997, 208.

35. For more on KTV in Taiwan, see J. Wu 1997.

36. KTV also had a sociospatial precedent in Taiwan called MTV (movie TV). MTV consists of rooms where friends can gather to watch a video in private. This quickly became a form of love motel for many, in which people who lived with their parents (ranging from teenagers to couples in their late twenties or early thirties) could go for trysts. Toward the end of the 1990s, MTV became less popular, but it was an important contribution to the rapid development of Taiwan's KTV industry.

37. Drew 2001, 74.

38. Ogawa 1998, 46.

39. Kelly 1998; Lum 1996, 9; Lum 1998, 168; Oba 2002, 225; Ogawa 1998, 54.

40. For more on this, see Boretz 2004, 178.

41. Baranovitch 2003, 46; D. Ceng 1999, 4; Condry 2006, 123; Drew 2001, 20; Ogawa 1998, 49.

42. Theo Chou, interview, December 19, 2005, Taipei. This interview was conducted in English.

43. "November's Chopin" (Shiyi yue de xiaobang).

44. Di Genova 2005, 18.

45. Baranovitch 2003, 46; L. Li 1993, 117. KTV works as advertising both in that one hears new songs that friends choose to sing and in reinforcing the popularity of one's favorite songs.

46. Claire Hsieh, interview, February 15, 2006, Taipei.

47. de Kloet 2001, 38–39.

48. Lum 1996, 64. See also, L. Li 1993, 116; Lum 1988.

49. Because of this private space, KTV also quickly split into two forms—one for friends to go for innocent fun, and a second that is a technological extension of hostess bars in which women are employed to sing, pour drinks, flirt, and encourage conversation. This can result in sexual activity after leaving the KTV—if the woman is so inclined and a suitable financial arrangement can be reached. Often, one KTV establishment can serve both functions in that one room might be occupied by friends or colleagues letting off steam at the end of the day, while an adjacent room in the same establishment might house men and their hostesses. For more on Taiwan's KTV as hostess bars, see Boretz 2004; Ōtake and Hosokawa 1998, 181.

50. In fact, in the early 1990s cram schools began opening that specifically catered

to honing karaoke skills (H. Wei 1992). Casey Lum, in his study of a Taiwanese community in the United States, noted that many people started taking singing lessons to better their karaoke performances (Lum 1996, 69). This also appears to be true for Japan as well. Shinobu Oku's work on middle-aged and older women in Japan suggests that in Japan women tend to win more karaoke competitions than men, prepare more, and show more interest in singing from a young age (Oku 1998, 56). In Oku's survey of middle-aged and older Japanese women who frequently went to karaoke, 7 percent responded that they never practiced, 30 percent said they often practiced, and 40 percent said they practiced every day (Oku 1998, 63). Further support for the importance of practice can be found in Hiroshi Ogawa's point that after karaoke appeared in Japan, CD singles often came with a karaoke accompaniment on the CD so people could practice singing at home (Ogawa 1998, 49).

51. See Drew 2001, 87; Lum 1996, 95–96.

52. Ivy 1995, 226.

53. This is perhaps especially useful for hostesses in preventing a reputation of being hardened money grabbers. Similarly, Eric Thompson suggests that an emphasis on romance helps to counter the negative images of Western/modern sexuality for Malay women (Thompson 2002, 71–72).

54. For more on this in other cultures outside of the karaoke context, see Sugarman 1989, 203. For more on the "socially mandatory" tears of women at wedding banquets as a performative context, see Adrian 2003, 182.

55. Sugarman 1989, 193, 203; Sugarman 1997, 339.

Chapter 2: China's Mandopop Roots and Taiwan's Gendered Counter-Invasion of the PRC

Epigraphs. Jones 1992, 3; Yang 2004, 230; Tanizaki 1928–1929.

1. For more on this, see Jones 2001, 30.

2. For more on this, see Jones 2001, 30–31.

3. For more on this, see Jones 2001, 25–33, and S. Zheng 1997, 92.

4. L. Lee 1999, 7.

5. Atkins 2001, 88.

6. P. Fu 1993, 48.

7. L. Lee 1999, 23–24.

8. Wakeman 1995, 10.

9. L. Lee 1999, 23–24.

10. For more on this, see L. Lee 1999, 34, and Wakeman 1995, 111. The movie *The White Countess* (Ivory 2005) also provides a nice feel for the plight of Russian exiles working in cabarettes in Shanghai in the period before the Japanese invasion.

11. Atkins 2001, 83–85; Jones 2001, 4–5; I. Wong 2002, 247; S. Zheng 1997.

12. L. Lee 1999, 83.

13. S. Zheng 1997, 93.

14. Jones 1992, 8.

15. For more on this in China, see Jones 2001, 54–55; in Japan, see Oba 2002, 233; and in Taiwan, see Jian and Guo 2004.

16. Wakeman 1995, 10.

17. Jones 2001, 55. The documentary *Viva Tonal!—The Dance Age* (*Tiaowu shidai*) forcefully demonstrates this point when they interview a man whose father used to sell the first gramophones in Yilan county on the east coast of Taiwan (Jian and Guo 2004). His father was selling a gramophone to a man who could not believe that there wasn't a band hiding inside. Tellingly, the man relating the story said, "My dad explained that it was an advanced product of civilization" (Jian and Guo 2004).

18. For more on this, see Atkins 2001, 65; Jian and Guo 2004; Jones 2001, 53.

19. Jones 2001, 62.

20. Jones 2001, 164.

21. Jones 2001, 165.

22. R. Chow 1991, 38.

23. For more on this, see I. Wong 2002, 249.

24. For more on this, see P. Fu 1993, 121; P. Fu 2003; Y. Ke and J. Zhang 1995, 75; L. Lee 1999, 328–330.

25. P. Fu 1993, 164. For a superb cinematic portrayal of this, see Ang Lee's movie *Lust, Caution* (2007).

26. S. Zheng 1997, 104.

27. Dujunco 2002, 25.

28. For more on this, see Jones and Hallet 1994, 453; Perris 1983, 13–18.

29. *Huerhaiya* has no meaning other than as a general cheer of enthusiasm.

30. For more on this, see Barmé 1987, 37.

31. For more on this, see Baranovitch 2003, 10.

32. Gerth forthcoming.

33. For more on this, see Baranovitch 2003, 12; Brace 1991, 45–49; W. Ho 2000, 343; S. Leng 1991, 30–31.

34. See de Kloet 2001, 182; Gold 1993, 915; Nonini and Ong 1997, 15; M. Yang 1997, 299–301, 309–310.

35. Alice, interview, July 6, 2006, Shanghai.

36. Baranovitch 2003, 12.

37. Gold 1993, 909.

38. Baranovitch 2003, 13.

39. Jay Chou, a Mandopop performer from Taiwan.

40. Jones 1992, 67.

41. Brace 1991, 45. See also Brace 1992.

42. For more on this, see Baranovitch 2003, 13; Gold 1993, 916–918; W. Ho 2000, 342; S. Leng 1991, 26.

43. For more on this, see Y. Chen 2000, 2–3.

44. Miss Li, interview, July 9, 2006, Shanghai.

45. For more on this, see H. Ceng 1997, 165; W. Ceng and L. Liu 1997, 144–145; H.

Chen 2002; Gold 1993, 908, 914, 925; Y. Ke 1993, 181–190; X. Zhang 1991, 86–87; Q. Zhou 1998, 122–123; Y. Zhu 2000, 211–214, 234, 296.

46. For more on this, see H. Ceng 1997, 167; Y. Ke 1993, 181–190; X. Zhang 1991, 86–87.

47. H. Ceng 1997, 167; Y. Ke and J. Zhang 1995, 110, 174–178; Y. Zhu 2000, 268–272.

48. Jones 1992, 17, 149.

49. Brace 1991, 43.

50. For more on the explicitly sexual nature of Shanghai's songs, see S. Zheng 1997.

51. See Baranovitch 2003, 15–16, 135; Brace 1991, 43; Honig and Hershatter 1988, 59–60, 70; Jones 2001; Jones 1992, 67–68; S. Leng 1991, 30; Witzleben 1999, 247.

52. Honig and Hershatter 1988, 61.

53. Jones 1992, 68.

54. W. Ho 2000, 342.

55. For more on this, see J. Zheng, Zhou, and Wu 2004, 164.

56. For more on songs of this era, see J. Zheng, Zhou, and Wu 2004, 164.

57. L. Li 1993, 18, 23.

58. J. Zheng, Zhou, and Wu 2004, 165.

59. Jones 1992, 79–81.

60. Baranovitch 2003, 194.

61. J. Zheng, Zhou, and Wu 2004, 166.

62. J. Zheng, Zhou, and Wu 2004, 166.

63. J. Zheng, Zhou, and Wu 2004, 166–169.

64. J. Zheng, Zhou, and Wu 2004, 168.

65. Baranovitch 2003, 194.

66. J. Zheng, Zhou, and Wu 2004, 167.

67. J. Zheng, Zhou, and Wu 2004, 166–167.

68. Baranovitch 2003, 202.

69. J. Zheng, Zhou, and Wu 2004, 174.

70. J. Zheng, Zhou, and Wu 2004, 133.

71. Perris 1983.

72. Baranovitch 2003, 196.

73. Baranovitch 2003, 201.

74. Baranovitch 2003, 196.

75. Baranovitch 2003, 214.

76. J. Zheng, Zhou, and Wu 2004.

77. J. Zheng, Zhou, and Wu 2004, 136.

78. Baranovitch 2003, 196.

79. Also see Y. Chen 2000, 174, ESWN 2006.

80. Baranovitch 2003, 227; de Kloet 2000, 243.

81. For more on this last point, see Witzleben 1999, 249.

82. For more on this in the PRC, see Jones 1992, 82. Ian Condry points out a similar discourse in Japan, as Japanese rockers claim authenticity compared to pop because they write their own lyrics and because of their grassroots base (Condry 2006, 122).

83. Efird 2001, 79.

84. de Kloet 2000, 242. See also Brace and Freidlander 1992.

85. H. Huang 2003, 193.

86. For more on this, see Efird 2001, 71.

87. For more on this, see Gold 1993, 919; H. Huang 2001, 6; H. Huang 2003, 191; Jones 1994, 158.

88. Baranovitch 2003, 42–44; H. Huang 2003, 193.

89. Baranovitch 2003, 36; de Kloet 2000, 244, 251.

90. H. Huang 2001, 6. For more on music and class in China, see R. Kraus 1989; G. Lee 1996.

91. Baranovitch 2003, 43–44.

92. Gold 1993, 921.

93. H. Huang 2001, 2.

94. Y. Zhang 1989. For more on this, see Baranovitch 2003, 24; Dujunco 2002, 30.

95. Baranovitch 2003, 20; Brace 1991, 49; Jones 1992, 68.

96. Dujunco 2002, 30.

97. L. Li 1993, 5.

98. H. Huang 2003, 194.

99. Baranovitch 2003, 49–50; Barmé 1987.

100. See Baranovitch 2003, 20–22, 130–131; Brace 1991, 49; de Kloet 2005a, 230–233; de Kloet 2005b, 611; de Kloet 2005c, 322–323; H. Huang 2003, 186, 195; Jones 1994, 159.

101. For more on this, see de Kloet 2005a, 230–233; de Kloet 2005b, 611; de Kloet 2005c, 322–323.

102. Amanda, interview, June 23, 2006, Shanghai.

103. Only two out of the eighteen people I interviewed in Shanghai viewed southern culture's feminine associations negatively.

104. Mr. Chen, interview, July 1, 2006, Shanghai.

105. Miss Wang, interview, July 3, 2006, Shanghai.

106. Christian, interview, July 4, 2006, Shanghai.

107. Mandopop also ushers in new conceptions of manhood, such as Jonathan Lee's song "I Am Ugly But I Am Tender" (*wenrou*) (L. Li 1993, 27), which sells images of sensitive new-age guys that contrast Beijing rock's masculinist ethos.

108. Moskowitz 2004; X. Zhang 1991, 85–86.

109. Baranovitch 2003, 115–116.

110. H. Huang 2003, 195

111. H. Huang 2001, 2.

112. Baranovitch 2003, 132, 143.

Chapter 3: Hybridity and Its Discontents

Epigraphs. Watson 1997b, 10; Twain 1869, 145.

1. *Chengpin shudian.*

2. Golden 2001.

3. *Renao*: Literally "hot and noisy," the hustle and bustle that makes life fun. For more on *renao*, see S.Yu 2004.

4. Taiwan was a Dutch colony from 1622 to 1661.

5. Y. Chen 1998, 54.

6. For more on this, see Y. Chen 1998, 84.

7. For more on this, see Y. Chen 1996, 36, and Y. Lü 2003, 131.

8. Y. Lü 2003, 133.

9. Y. Chen 1998, 84; Y. Lü 2003, 177.

10. Jian and Guo 2004; W. Tsai 2002a, 6–7.

11. See Y. Chen 1996, 53; Jian and Guo 2004; Y. Ke and J. Zhang 1995, 71; Y. Lü 2003, 139; Z. Su 1999, 2; W. Tsai 2002a, 7.

12. Jian and Guo 2004; W. Tsing 2002a, 9.

13. Jian and Guo 2004.

14. Jian and Guo 2004.

15. Jian and Guo 2004.

16. As with Mandopop today, Peking opera was not without its controversies—Taiwan's press warned of its "evil effects," for example (Jian and Guo 2004).

17. Y. Lü 2003, 141; L. Ye 2001, 81.

18. L. Ye 2001, 80. Highlighting this fact, Eva Airlines used the song in its advertisements as a conscious political statement to align itself with Taiwan rather than choosing a Mandarin Chinese song as with China Airlines (Shuenn-Der Yu, personal communication, January 5, 2006).

19. Lu Hanxiu has stated that, more than any other song, its title is used in magazine articles and television programs and points out that in 1977 a movie bearing the same name was produced that followed the outline of the song's lyrics (H. Lu 2003, 62). Lu also suggests that the song also captured Taiwan's eager anticipation of its future in an era of great progress (H. Lu 2003, 61).

20. Y. Lü 2003, 142.

21. Jian and Guo 2004.

22. For more on this, see Jian and Guo 2004.

23. For more on this, see Y. Chen 1996, 62; W. Tsai 2002a, 13. During the Pacific War, people in Taiwan had to use bamboo needles because all the copper and iron needles had to be melted down for the war effort. Bamboo needles actually produced a less scratchy sound than their metal counterparts, but the bamboo needles wore down quickly (Jian and Guo 2004).

24. For more on this, see Jian and Guo 2004. At that time Japan had seized China's coastal territory and Japanese-language songs about mainland China also became popular (Jian and Guo 2004).

25. W. Tsai 2002a, 13.

26. W. Tsai 2002a, 17–19.

27. W. Tsai 1992b, 22.

28. Y. Yeh 1995, 10. The government also created laws that stated that the record companies had the rights to a song before releasing it, resulting in many of the most talented

lyricists and composers leaving the music industry because it paid so little (W. Tsai 1992b, 22).

29. Y. Lü 2003, 203.

30. I. Yang 1992, 58.

31. G. Wang 1986, 367; I. Yang 1992, 54.

32. For more on this, see G. Wang 1986, 367; I. Yang 1993, 97; Y. Yeh 1995, 11.

33. Y. Lü 2003, 203.

34. M. Zhang 1997, 55.

35. Y. Yeh 1995, 12; C. Zhang 2003, 190.

36. Y. Yeh 1995, 12; C. Zhang 2003, 190.

37. Y. Yeh 1995, 13.

38. For more on this, see H. Ceng 1998, 179; Y. Lü 2003, 202; I. Yang 1992, 59.

39. G. Wang 1986, 367.

40. I. Yang 1992, 62–63. Nature imagery is still quite common in contemporary Mandopop, though it is usually used to describe settings rather than as an allusion to a love relationship itself.

41. For more on this, see I. Yang 1992, 57.

42. For more on class alignment with Japanese *enka*, see Yano 2000, 62.

43. Mrs. Lu, interview, September 1, 1999, Taipei.

44. Though the term *enka* only came about in the late 1960s and early 1970s (Tansman 1996, 111), Japanese *enka* was created in the Meiji era (Stanlaw 2000, 77; Tansman 1996, 111; Yano 2003, 28). A musical form that today is thought to be distinctively Japanese, *enka* was at its inception in the Meiji period a heavily Western-influenced genre that adopted, and adapted, Western musical instruments such as the guitar and drums for its own use. As Japan became more nationalistic before and during the Second World War, *enka* had already become indigenized enough that it was taken as an acceptable nationalistic alternative to American-based jazz and pop (Yano 2003, 37). The fact that it too had many foreign influences, including the use of Western instruments, was largely ignored (Yano 2003, 37).

45. Yano 2000, 60.

46. For more on *enka* in relation to these themes, see Ivy 1995, 224.

47. I. Yang 1993, 97, 108.

48. Wu Bai has also been called the "godfather" of Taiwan's rock scene (de Kloet 2005a, 234).

49. As a point of contrast, singer/songwriter Bobby Chen used Hokkien words in his songs long before Wu Bai had become popular. Yet Bobby Chen's Hokkien accent, I am told, sounds both urban and northern. Bobby Chen's use of Hokkien thus becomes a peace offering—an olive branch for different ethnic groups in Taiwan. Yet however well-intentioned, his efforts are commonly dismissed as a top-down offer of cooperation and as such the political force of such a gesture is undermined.

50. Chang Cheng Yue, interview, March 9, 2006.

51. Difang Duana was paid very little, and eventually won a lawsuit against Enigma. For more on this, see Guy 2001, 2002a, 2002b. Bobby Chen incorporates the same aboriginal melody in his song "Happy Reunion" (Huanju ge) with aboriginal, Hakka, Mandarin,

and Taiwanese verses. Bobby Chen won the best composer award in the 1996 Golden Melody Awards for this song.

52. Ms. Meng, interview, November 28, 2005.

53. This, in turn, is part of a larger movement in Taiwan to promote aboriginal tourism in the name of Taiwanese identity, but which has usually led to a mere commodification of racial otherness with little cultural meaning preserved.

54. I. Yang 1992, 64. This stands in stark contrast with the highly politicized music industry in the PRC.

55. Many people I have interviewed have emphasized that soap operas are largely responsible for Taiwan's love of Japanese and Korean pop music. For more on Japanese and Korean soap operas in relation to their pop music, see H. Liang 2001, 178; Ogawa 2004, 149–152. Hongbin Liang attributes Taiwan's rap scene as beginning when Xu Huaiyu began performing Korean rap melodies with Chinese lyrics in 1997 (H. Liang 2001, 176). Liang also suggests that Taiwan's R&B was inspired by Japanese and Korean pop (H. Liang 2001, 178).

56. Iwabuchi 2002, 32–33.

57. K. Lo 2001, 263; D. Wu 1997, 135.

58. de Kloet 2001, 180.

59. de Kloet 2003, 25.

60. For more on this, see A. Chun 2004, 50; A. Chun and Rossiter 2004, 2; L. Ching 2001, 305–306.

61. Shuker 1994, 62.

62. Iwabuchi 2002, 200; A. Ong 1999, 119–121.

63. A-Guai Chen, interview, November 27, 2006, Taipei.

64. Miss Luo and Mr. Onion, interview, July 12, 2004, Taipei.

65. Valen Hsu, interview, October 23, 2005, Taipei.

66. Baranovitch 2003; Brace 1991, 49.

67. Lipsitz 2001, 189.

68. Tim, interview, October 18, 2005, Taipei.

69. Xiangyu, interview, November 20, 2003, Taipei.

70. Aoyagi 2000, 321.

71. *Waipo* (maternal grandmother).

72. Appadurai 1996, 77–78.

73. Stefanie Sun, interview, October 23, 2005, Taipei.

74. Lai and Mok 1981, 47.

75. Lai and Mok 1981, 48.

76. Thompson 2002, 59.

77. Thompson 2002, 59–60. Thompson goes on to explore the intriguing possibility that Malaysian pop uses paradox and irony to reject the very Western form that inspired its origins, thereby emphasizing its position as a new genre (Thompson 2002, 62).

78. Adrian 2003, 13–14; Bhabha 1994; Taussig 1993.

79. For Disneyland in Japan, see Raz 1999; Van Maanen 1992. For Kentucky Fried Chicken, see Iwabuchi 2002. For McDonalds in East Asia, see J. Ho 1994; Ohnuki-Tierney

1997; Watson 1997a; D. Wu 1997. For Mickey Mouse in Japan, see Van Maanen 1992. For sports in China and Taiwan, see Brownell 1995; Morris 2002, 2004a, 2004b. For Japanese hip-hop, see Condry 2001.

80. Rosenberger 2001, 151.
81. Thompson 2002, 62.
82. Bhabha 1994; Taussig 1993.
83. Bhabha 1994; Taussig 1993.
84. Manuel 1988, 221.
85. Condry 2006, 151; Stanlaw 1992, 73–74.
86. De Launey 1995, 221.
87. De Launey 1995, 221.
88. Mr. Tao, interview, August 5, 2003, Taipei.
89. Atkins 2000, 31.
90. Atkins 2000, 51.
91. As an example, Atkins cites indigenous transformations of music such as the Japanese introduction of space (quiet moments between notes) that transform American jazz into distinctly Japanese (Atkins 2000, 41; Atkins 2001, 258). The use of the bamboo flute in Japanese jazz is another example (Atkins 2000, 40).
92. Iwabuchi 2002, 40, 105.
93. Hebdige 1987; Sanjek 2001, 245–246.
94. Goodwin 1992, 83.
95. Lipsitz 1994, 162–164.
96. Frith 1988, 6.
97. Lipsitz 1994, 165–167.
98. Lipsitz 1994, 167.
99. For more on club culture in Taiwan, see Moskowitz 2008.
100. Winnie, interview, October 28, 2003, Taipei.
101. Miss Cai, interview, August 1, 1999, Taipei.
102. Xiangyu, interview, November 20, 2003, Taipei.
103. Valen Hsu, interview, October 23, 2005, Taipei.
104. In the early 1990s, Japan's recording industry and market was second only to the United States in worldwide gross sales, for example (Yano 2003, 46).
105. Treat 1996, 13.
106. Bennett 2000, 52.

Chapter 4: Message in a Bottle

Epigraphs. Dickens 1861, 136; Morrison 1987, 71; de Saint-Exupéry 1943, 58.
1. Y. Jiang 2006. The same study found that people between the ages of twenty and twenty-four, or above seventy, were the most lonely (Y. Jiang 2006).
2. For more on this, see Moskowitz 2007.
3. J. Wu 1985, 136.
4. Adrian 2003, 93.

5. Adrian 2003, 93–98.

6. Adrian 2003, 94. This reflects a general dissatisfaction with marriage but also that women have greater economic independence than they once did, so they are not bound to unhappy marriages.

7. Adrian 2003, 94.

8. A. Lee 2004a; A. Lee 2004b, 125–129.

9. A. Lee 2004a; A. Lee 2004b, 112–117; Moskowitz 2007.

10. Simon 2003.

11. Simon 2003, 109.

12. Simon 2003, 113.

13. For example, see Liu and Liang 2003, 5–6; J. Wu 1985, 122.

14. Hermalin, Liu, and Freeman 1994, 56.

15. Adrian 2003, 33; Hermalin, Liu, and Freeman 1994, 56.

16. Wolf 1968, 1972.

17. V. Lee 2007a, 84.

18. V. Lee 2007a, 89.

19. V. Lee 2007a; V. Lee 2007b.

20. There were 16,779 suicides from 2001 to 2005, for example, with 4,282 of them in 2005 alone (V. Lee 2007b, 89). For more on women and suicide in China, see Wolf 1975.

21. J. Wu 1985, 31.

22. J. Wu 1985, 146.

23. Hanser 2002, 190–193.

24. H. Huang 2003, 185.

25. H. Huang 2003, 185. Huang is quoting Chinese academics here.

26. Baranovitch 2003, 49–50; Hanser 2002, 195–201.

27. Levy 2002.

28. Y. Zhao 2002.

29. Y. Zhao 2002.

30. G. Lee 1995, 96.

31. H. Huang 2001, 10.

32. Baranovitch 2003, 43–44.

33. Bellah et al. 1985.

34. Bellah et al. 1985.

35. J. Wu 1985, 130.

36. Mr. Tao, interview, July 2002, Taipei.

37. Atkins 2001, 40; Oba 2002, 240.

38. W. Chen 1996.

39. Keane 2002, 129.

40. J. Wu 1985, 119.

41. Miss Yan, interview, June 23, 2006, Shanghai.

42. Miss Dai, interview, August 3, 1999, Taipei.

43. de Kloet 2001, 121.

44. This accounts for a two-week period for February 2006. G-Music. 2006. "G-

music Billboard Chart Based on Sales from 2/3/06–2/9/06, A Combination of Rose Records (Meigui changpian), Dazhong Records (Dazhong changpian), and G-music." www.g-music .com.tw/GMusicBillboard1.aspx (accessed February 11, 2006).

45. As with the Mandopop chart, this accounted for the most popular songs, regardless of musical genre. Bilboard.biz. 2005. "US Pop Charts." www.billboard.biz/bb/biz/ yarendcharts/2005/tlptitl.jsp.

46. A chart that I compiled in 2002 from a different company's billboard charts bore similar results, for example. Rose Records 2002. "Taiwan Top 20 " www.roserecords.com.tw.

47. Literally "his shadow."

48. "Tears" is also a prevalent key word in these songs. Because Christine Yano has covered this aspect of Japanese *enka* so well (Yano 2003, 98–102), however, I will not repeat her analysis here.

49. Similarly, although the song does not use the word "kiss," there is an implied intimacy through the presence of her tears on his face.

50. Stefanie Sun, interview, October 23, 2005, Taipei.

51. Miss Su, interview, January 9, 2006, Taipei.

52. Chang Cheng Yue, interview, March 9, 2006, Taipei.

53. Miss Su, interview, January 9, 2006, Taipei.

54. George Trivino, interview, March 9, 2006, Taipei.

55. S. Huang 2000, 6.

56. Miss Guo, interview, October 12, 2003, Taipei.

57. Yano 2003, 3. See also S. Chan 1997.

58. Maria, interview, August 23, 2003, Taipei.

59. Henderson 1996.

60. For more on Mandopop's Buddhist emphasis on accepting fate, see Y. Ke and J. Zhang 1995, 117; Z. Su 1999, 80; and I. Yang 1996, 9.

61. Mrs. Chen, interview, October 24, 2003, Taipei.

62. Y. Ke and J. Zhang 1995, 131–132.

63. Y. Ke and J. Zhang 1995, 138.

64. Mr. Chen, interview, July 1, 2006, Shanghai.

65. Xiangyu, interview, November 20, 2003, Taipei.

66. Hou Hsiao-hsien's movie *Three Times* (H. Hou 2005) has a wonderful scene in which the protagonist gives a music tape to the heroine to express his unspoken feelings for her.

67. Miss Fu, interview, July 7, 2006, Shanghai.

68. Miss Zhou, interview, July 5, 2002, Taipei.

69. Buxton 1983, 431.

Chapter 5: Men Writing Songs for Women Who Complain about Men

Epigraphs. Woolf 1928, 113; Frith 1996, 274.

1. When I asked people in Taiwan if women wrote songs for men, the only example

they could provide was the female performer Wawa, who regularly co-writes David Tao's lyrics. David Tao's Los Angeles origins and lack of Chinese fluency may have influenced his choice in having Wawa co-write his songs. No doubt there are other examples, yet it is significant that no one I spoke with could think of them, though these same people could effortlessly list male lyricists who wrote for women.

2. For more on this, see S. Zheng 1997, 115.

3. For more on gender bending in Chinese opera, see S. Li 2003; Silvio 1998.

4. See Moskowitz 2004.

5. Moskowitz 2004; Silvio 1998, 187–190.

6. S. Li 2003.

7. H. Liu 1999, 113; Z. Su 1999, 36.

8. H. Ceng 1997, 165, 179; H. Liu 1999, 6–7; Z. Su 1999, 35.

9. H. Liu 1999, 4–7.

10. H. Liu 1999, 6–7; Z. Su 1999, 35.

11. For more on this issue in Republican China, see Dikötter 1995. For more on this in the PRC, see Evans 1997; Honig and Hershatter 1988, 15–17. For more on this in Taiwan, see Moskowitz 2001, 2004.

12. For more on this, see Y. Ke and J. Zhang 1995, 110–111; Z. Su 1999, 51, 70, 90; P. Xiao and Z. Su 2002, 183.

13. Z. Su 1999, 77.

14. H. Ceng 1997, 165; Y. Ke and J. Zhang 1995; H. Liu 1999, 61, 83.

15. For more on specific terms that are used to describe men and women, see H. Ceng 1997, 177; Y. Ke and J. Zhang 1995, 112–113, 115, 122, 124–125, 148, 174, 177, 179; H. Liu 1999, 34, 55–57, 83; Z. Su 1999, 82–88, 96; I. Yang 1993, 103–104; P. Xiao and Z. Su 2002, 189; X. Zhang 1991, 85; Y. Zhu 2000, 271.

16. Y. Ke and J. Zhang 1995, 124–125, 138; P. Xiao and Z. Su 2002, 181; Y. Zhu 2000, 269.

17. Hermalin, Liu, and Freeman 1994, 56.

18. Adrian 2003, 33; Hermalin, Liu, and Freeman 1994, 56.

19. Y. Ke and J. Zhang 1995, 147–148. For more on the cultural dynamics of having men leave while women stayed in the villages, see M. Wolf 1968, 1972.

20. C. Zhang 2003, 199.

21. For more on this, see Reheja and Gold 1994.

22. For more on this, see I. Wong 2002.

23. For more on women sucking the life out of men, see Moskowitz 2001, 2004; van Gulik 1961. For more on the dangerous spiritual pollution of women, see Ahern 1975; Seaman 1981. For more on women as all-powerful deities, see Sangren 1993, 1996, 2000; Seaman 1981.

24. Y. Ke and J. Zhang 1995, 158–162.

25. Y. Ke 1993, 185; H. Liu 1999, 61; Y. Ke and J. Zhang 1995, 112.

26. For more on the argument that women's images are being shaped by men in Japan, see Stanlaw 2000, 78, and Yano 2003, 5, 57, 149. For more on portraying women for men's

pleasure in Chinese culture, see Y. Ke and J. Zhang 1995, 136, 175; H. Liu 1999; Z. Su 1999, 35, 82–83, 88. For more on men usurping women's power through lyrical production in the PRC, see Baranovitch 2003, 155.

27. Moskowitz 2004; X. Zhang 1991, 85. Similarly shifting versions of manhood can also be found in modern cinema (see Moskowitz 2004).

28. J. Wong 1997; V. Wong 1998b.

29. For more on this, see H. Ceng 1997, 37; Y. Shih 2004, 1; C. Zhang 2003, 213–214; S. Zheng 1992, 58. Critics of Mandopop also tend to see Lee as the central force in Mandopop's role in enforcing sexist gender roles (See H. Ceng 1997, 165, 169–171, 177–179; H. Liu 1992, 16).

30. She had produced other albums before this but they did not do well.

31. Everyone I spoke with seemed very familiar with her life.

32. Y. Zhu 2000, 272.

33. The CD translates this song as "Suffer for You." I use a more literal translation because the same phrase recurs in the song's lyrics and because the imagery of the Chinese title is more vivid.

34. Elaine, interview, August 7, 2005, Taipei.

35. P. Xiao and Z. Su 2002, 189; I. Yang 1993, 103–104. Several of the women I interviewed also mentioned this.

36. Y. Ke and J. Zhang 1995, 117; Z. Su 1999, 80.

37. Q. Chen 1997, 39–40.

38. X. Zhang 1991.

39. The word *weidao* has several different nuances. It usually refers to "scent" in this song, but it also commonly refers to "atmosphere" or "feeling" (of a restaurant, bar, etc.), which I think is a better fit in this instance. The fact that the lyricist can employ the different nuances of the same word in one song is part of his demonstration of a creative command of the language that adds to the sophistication of the lyrics.

40. Mrs. Chen, interview, February 4, 1999, Taipei.

41. Personal communication, November 19, 2003, Taipei.

42. Elaine, interview, August 19, 2004, Taipei.

43. Little Mei and Little Hong, interview, July 3, 2006, Shanghai.

44. Angel, interview, October 12, 2003, Taipei.

45. Several of the people I interviewed also suggested that many of the songwriters are gay and therefore understand women's hearts by virtue of their more feminine natures. This naturalizes the homosexual male as an identity somewhere in between the categories of heterosexual male and heterosexual female.

46. Gerth 2003.

47. Honig and Hershatter 1988.

48. Dikötter 1995; Moskowitz 2001.

49. Andrews and Shen 2002; I. Wong 2002, 252–253.

50. S. Zheng 1997, 106.

51. Baranovitch 2003, 108; Honig and Hershatter 1988.

52. Baranovitch 2003, 12.

53. For an examination of the shifting nature of pictorial representations of women, see Andrews and Shen 2002; Hooper 1994.

54. Baranovitch 2003, 108, 144–147; Honig and Hershatter 1988.

55. For more on Taiwanese women mediating between different expectations, see Moskowitz 2007, 2008.

56. She is currently living in the United States.

57. Miss Li, Miss Yang, and Mr. Zhang, interview, July 15, 2005, Taipei.

58. It also reflects on the relative exclusion of Taiwanese aborigines from university education and white-collar jobs that results in a higher percentage of aboriginal women engaging in prostitution.

59. For more on this, see Guy 2002a. Looking at A-mei's images over the years, it is also arguable that she has become more modest in her attire as she has become more associated with the symbol of Taiwan's national identity.

60. Blum 2001, 78; Hyde 2001; Schein 2000.

61. Condry 2006, 164–171.

62. For more on girl bands' body images in Taiwan, see H. Chen 2002.

63. O. Chung 2005, 6.

64. See Witzleben 1999, 247.

65. See Fung and Curtin 2002.

66. Friedberg 2001, 155.

67. Napier 2001, 12.

68. Thompson 2002, 71.

69. See H. Ceng 1997, 165, 169–171; H. Liu 1999; Y. Ke and J. Zhang 1995, 113; P. Xiao and Z. Su 2002, 189–190.

Chapter 6: A Man for All Occasions

Epigraph. Haruki Murakami 1980, 321; *Sounds of Love and Sorrow*, dir. Hu Tai-li, 2000.

1. For more on the romanticization of the *wenrou* male in Hong Kong cinema, including images of Leslie Cheung, see Moskowitz 2004.

2. Bordo 1993.

3. For more on the association of Western musculature with barbarianism in contrast to the more slender "civilized" Chinese or Taiwanese, see Andrew Morris on Taiwan (2004a) or Susan Brownell on the PRC (1995). This in turn is linked to Chinese perceptions of other physical characteristics, such as hairiness, as signifying that Westerners are closer to animals (Dikötter 1997; Watson 1998).

4. I. Yang 1993, 99–101; I. Yang 1996, 11. Sheryl Garratt makes a similar point for Western pop music (Garratt 1984, 406). Irene Yang also suggests that these songs promise eternal love to assuage the confusion of real-life impermanent relationships (I. Yang 1993, 102).

5. Frith 1988, 169.

6. Garratt 1984, 402.

7. Yuanyuan, interview, August 16, 2005, Taipei.

8. Given the content of the song it is likely that Yuanyuan is correct that Mrs. Lu was thinking of Richie Jen's image rather than the particular song that she cited.

9. Vivian, interview, August 26, 2005, Taipei.

10. *Zhengzhao* refers to "symptoms," which seems more in keeping with the other medical themes of the song. The word can also refer to "signs" or "omens," which also adds nuance to the ominous feel of the song.

11. Literally, the glitter of youthful eyes (*nianqing de yanzhong muguang shanshuo*).

12. Sharman 1975.

13. Another example is Chang Cheng Yue's song "0204 I" about an adult phone line that every single man should have, but that he'd better "hurry up" because the toll is so expensive.

14. Mr. Zhang, interview, July 15, 2005, Taipei.

15. Although this interview was conducted in Chinese, he said "girl power" in English.

16. Chang Cheng Yue, interview, March 9, 2006, Taipei.

17. Ortner 1974. For more on this in Republican China, see Dikötter 1995. Honig and Hershatter also address this for the PRC (1988).

18. She performs in restaurants, small bars, and other venues. She does not have any CDs.

19. Becky, interview, October 17, 2005, Taipei.

20. For more on this, see Aoyagi 2000, 311; Condry 2006, 166.

21. W. Lau 2002.

22. Y. Zhang 2007.

23. de Kloet 2001, 122.

24. Dyer 1979, 415.

25. Dyer 1979, 416.

26. For more on this in familial and religious contexts, see Moskowitz 2001.

Chapter 7: Mandopop Under Siege

Epigraphs. Drake 2003, 76; Ching 1995, 271; Hennion 1983, 205.

1. These statements have been documented in the following scholarship: Baranovitch 2003, 15–16, 135; Brace 1991, 43, 59; Fung and Curtin 2002, 265; Gold 1993, 92; Honig and Hershatter 1988, 59–60, 70; Jones 2001; S. Leng 1991, 30; Witzleben 1999, 247.

2. Honig and Hershatter 1988, 61.

3. S. Leng 1991, 25.

4. Johnson 1983; Stacey 1983.

5. For more in this, see Baranovitch 2003, 20–22, 130–131; Brace 1991, 49; de Kloet 2005a, 230–233; de Kloet 2005b, 611; de Kloet 2005c, 322–323; H. Huang 2003, 186, 195; Jones 1994, 159. Of course, this overlooks the Western origins of rock as well as contemporary Beijing rock stars' conscious efforts to employ imagery that identifies them with Western rock (see Efird 2001, 71).

6. ESWN 2006.

7. ESWN 2006.

8. M. Yang 1997, 310.

9. See H. Liang 2001, 179.

10. X. Liu 1984, 172.

11. X. Liu 1984, 170.

12. X. Liu 1984, 170.

13. X. Liu 1984, 170.

14. Xiangyu, interview, November 20, 2003, Taipei.

15. Appadurai 1996, 41; Hobsbawm 1997a, 1997b; Kondo 1990, 74; Ohnuki-Tierney 1993, 4. For more on nostalgia in the popular music itself, see Taylor 2004.

16. Appadurai 1996, 77; Iwabuchi 2002, 174.

17. See H. Ceng 1997, 169–171; Y. Ke and J. Zhang 1995, 113; H. Liu 1999, 61, 83; Z. Su 1999, 36; P. Xiao and Z. Su 2002, 189–190. For assertions that the music is sexist without reference to youth consumption, see H. Liu 1992, 16.

18. See Hebdige 1979, 1987, for example.

19. Momphard 2003, 16.

20. Drake 2003, 77.

21. L. Ching 1995, 272.

22. Robinson et al. 1991.

23. Robinson et al. 1991, 3.

24. Robinson et al. 1991, 140.

25. Chun and Rossiter 2004, 13.

26. Robinson et al. 1991, 140–141.

27. See Brenner 1998, 10; Harrell 1994, 166; Honig and Hershatter 1988, 7–8; A. Ong 1999, 53.

28. I. Yang 1992, 59.

29. Theo Chou, interview, December 19, 2005. This interview was conducted in English.

30. Chen Xiaojuan wrote the melody of this song and won the Golden Melody Award for best melody. Li Zhuoxiong wrote the lyrics and also won the Golden Melody Award for best lyrics. It is interesting that Xiangyu is taking this song to represent Chen Xiaojuan's life when Li Zhuxiong wrote the lyrics. Her basic point, that many felt Karen Mok won the Golden Melody Award because of her talented songwriters rather than her own skills, however, is valid, though personally I think Karen Mok's voice gives the song a distinctive style which adds to the song.

31. Xiangyu, interview, November 20, 2003.

32. Michelle, interview, October 28, 2003, Taipei.

33. Tanaka 1998, 121.

34. Becker 2001, 68.

35. Kealy 1979.

36. Adorno 1941.

37. Benjamin 1955. Benjamin qualified his statements and indeed was perhaps the

first voice to suggest a mimetic subversion of audiences, but I would argue that the overall tone of his work is more mistrustful of popular culture than revisionist theories acknowledge.

38. Habermas 1989.

39. Such as Dick Hebdige's remorse over the standardization of once alternative musical forms in England as becoming "frozen" over time (Hebdige 1979, 96).

40. Frith 1996, 9.

41. Dyer 1979, 411, 417–418.

42. de Kloet 2003, 25; Dyer 1979, 411–412.

43. de Kloet 2003, 25.

44. Dyer 1979, 412.

45. Dyer 1979, 412.

46. Dyer 1979, 413.

47. For punk, see Hebdige 1979. For rock and roll, see Frith 1988.

48. Dyer 1979; Stokes 2004, 32.

49. Frith 1996, 69.

50. Cawelti 2001, 205.

51. Fiske 2001.

52. Fiske 2001, 218.

53. Goodwin 1988, 260.

54. This includes Americans, Canadians, French, and Germans.

55. D. Ceng quantifies this by stating that Mandopop audiences' musical choices are based approximately 30 percent on the melody and 70 percent on the lyrics (D. Ceng 1999, 7).

56. For more on this issue in relation to heavy metal, see Weinstein 1991, 273. For more on this in relation to soap operas, see Allen 2001, 239.

57. Allen 2001, 239.

58. L. Ching 1995, 280.

59. Miss Cai, interview, November 1, 2003, Taipei.

60. Miss Luo, interview, July 12, 2004, Taipei.

61. Miss Li, interview, July 9, 2006, Shanghai.

62. George Trivino, interview, March 9, 2006, Taipei.

63. The possessive marker "de."

64. See J. Ho 1994; Morris 2002, 2004a, 2004b; Ohnuki-Tierney 1997; Raz 1999; Van Maanen 1992; Watson 1997a, 1997b, 1997c; D. Wu 1997, among others.

65. Geertz 1973, 18.

66. Farrer 2002, 30.

Glossary

Beijing rock
China's rock and roll epicenter is in Beijing, in the north of China. Beijing rock is part of a gendered discourse in which the north of China is associated with masculinized music and the south (Taiwan, Hong Kong, and, in more recent years, Shanghai) is associated with the more popular feminine-associated Mandopop.

campus songs
A folk song movement in Taiwan from 1977 to 1981. The campus song movement was an attempt to create local popular music but it was often saturated with pan-Chinese themes rather than local Taiwanese identities. This musical movement quickly spread to Hong Kong.

Cantopop
Cantonese pop music. All uses of the term Cantopop in this book refer to music produced in Hong Kong.

DPP
Democratic Progressive Party. Chen Shui-Bian was the first DPP member to become president (2000–2008). The DPP has traditionally been associated with a pro-Taiwan independence stance.

Gang-Tai pop
Music from Hong Kong (XiangGANG) and Taiwan (TAIwan). The term is only heard in the PRC because people in Taiwan, Hong Kong, and other regions outside of China proper see large distinctions between Hong Kong and Taiwan pop. In most cases, the use of the term Gang-Tai pop therefore signifies the opinions of people in the PRC about Mandopop produced outside of its borders.

KMT
The Kuomintang government. After losing China to the communist revolution in 1949, the KMT established itself in Taiwan. The KMT has traditionally been seen as wanting reunification with China were the political conditions acceptable.

KTV
Taiwan-style karaoke in which friends gather to sing in a private room rather than in a public venue such as a bar (as is usually the case in the United States).

Mandopop   Mandarin Chinese pop music.

PRC   The People's Republic of China. The government in China since 1949.

PRC pop   Mandopop produced in the PRC. To date, PRC pop only accounts for an extremely small part of the Mandopop market.

revolutionary disco   Revolutionary disco can be found in the PRC. In the mid-1980s, revolutionary songs, including "The East Is Red," were reissued with a new disco beat.

Taiyupop   Hokkien dialect pop music produced in Taiwan. This has also been referred to as Hokkiopop in other scholarship.

Taiwan pop   Mandopop produced in Taiwan.

tongsu music   *Tongsu* music (*tongsu yinyue*), meaning "music for the masses," is found in the PRC. It is very distinctive from Mandopop in that *tongsu* focuses on socialist ideals and praise of the state.

wenrou   Usually translated into English as "tender," *wenrou* connotes a gentle, caring, and self-sacrificing person. When this term is used to describe men, it often has the connotations of what would in the West be termed as effeminate.

yuanfen   The idea that people are destined to have emotional relationships in this life because they knew each other in past lives. This traditional Buddhist concept can often be found in modern Mandopop.

xibeifeng   *Xibeifeng* (the northwest wind), a musical movement of the mid-1980s, is found in the PRC. *Xibeifeng* is heavily tied into the film industry, getting its start in movies such as Zhang Yimou's *Red Sorghum* (1989). Like *tongsu* music, it was introduced by the state-controlled music industry in an attempt to wrest cultural hegemony from the hands of Taiwan and Hong Kong.

Discography

Bu, Wancang, dir. 1931. "The Peach Blossom Weeps Blood" (*Taohua qixieji*). Shanghai: Lianhua Film Company.

Chang, Cheng Yue. 1998. "Let's Break Up" (Fenshou ba). In *Secret Base of Operations* (*Mimi jidi*). Taipei: Moyan Records.

———. 2000. "Male and Female Dog" (Gou nan nü). In *Problemed* (*You wenti*). Taipei: Moyan Records.

———. 2000. "Think Too Much" (Xiang tai duo). In *Problemed* (*You wenti*). Taipei: Moyan Records.

———. 2000. "0204 I." In *Problemed* (*You wenti*). Taipei: Moyan Records.

Chan, Jackie (Cheng Long). 1996. "How Can It Be?" (Zeme hui?). In *Dragon's Heart*, Jackie Chan (*Long de xin*, Jackie Chan). Taipei: Rock Records.

Chen, Bobby (Chen Sheng). 1995. "Happy Reunion" (Huanju ge). In *New Treasure Island Entertainment Troup Album 3* (*Xin baodao kangledui di san ji*). Taipei: Rock Records.

Chou, Jay (Zhou Jielun). 2003. "Terraced Field" (Titian). In *Ye hui mei*. Taipei: Warner Music.

———. 2003. "Third Grade, Class Two" (San nian er ban). In *Ye hui mei*. Taipei: Warner Music.

———. 2005. *November's Chopin* (*Shiyi yue de xiaobang*). Taipei: Warner Music.

Chun, Chun. 1932. "The Peach Blossom Weeps Blood" (Taohua qixieji). Taipei: Columbia Records.

———. 1933. "Facing the Spring Breeze" (Wang chunfeng). Taipei: Columbia Records.

Cranberries, The. 1993. "Dreams." In *Everybody Else is Doing It So Why Can't We?* Dublin: Polygram Records.

Dong, Wenhua. 1999. "The Great Wall of China Is Long" (*Changchen Chang*). In "The Great Wall of China Is Long" (*Changchen Chang*). Beijing: Fengya Record Company.

Enigma. 1998. "Return to Innocence." In *The Cross of Changes*. Los Angeles: EMI International.

Feng, Feifei. 1982. "I Am Chinese" (Wo shi Zhongguoren). In *I Am Chinese* (*Wo shi Zhongguoren*). Taipei: Gelin Record Company.

Hsin, Winnie (Xin Xiaoqi). 1994. "Realization" (Lingwu). In *Scent* (*Weidao*). Taipei: Rock International MS Publ.

———. 1994. "Scent" (Weidao). In *Scent* (*Weidao*). Taipei: Rock International MS Publ.

Hsu, Valen (Xu Ruyun). 2007. *Latitude 66 Degrees* (66 Pohjoista Leveyttä, *Beiwei liushiliu du*). Taipei: Seed Music.

Jen, Richie (Ren Xinqi). 1996. "A Heart That Is Too Soft" (Xin tai ruan). In *A Heart That Is Too Soft* (*Xin tai ruan*). Taipei: Rock Records.

Lam, Sandy (Lin Yilian). 1995. "Because of You I Am Blown by a Cold Wind" (Wei ni wo shou leng feng chui). In *Love, Sandy*. Taipei: Rock International MS Pub.

———. 1995. "Scars." In *Love, Sandy*. Taipei: Rock Records.

Lee, Jonathan (Li Zongshen). 1987. "I Have Something to Say" (Wo you hua yao shuo). In *I Have Something to Say* (*Wo you hua yao shuo*). Taipei: Rock Records.

———. 1999. "Seventeen Year Old Girl's *Wenrou*" (Shiqi sui nüsheng de wenrou). In *Jonathan Lee's Anthology* (*Zuopin Li Zongshen*). Taipei: Rock Records.

Liu Huan. 2000. "The Valiant Spirit of Asia" (*Yazhou xiongfeng*). In *The Valiant Spirit of Asia* (*Yazhou xiongfeng*). Beijing: Shanghua Record Company.

Mitchell, Joni. 1974. "People's Parties." In *Court and Spark*. Los Angeles: Electra Music.

Mok, Karen (Mo Wenwei). 2002. "Love" (Ai). In Karen Mok ([i] *Mo Wenwei* [i]). Taipei: Sony Music Entertainment Taiwan.

Qi Yu. 1979. "Olive Tree" (Ganlanshu). In *Olive Tree* (*Ganlanshu*). Taipei: Synco Cultural Corporation.

Sun, Stefanie (Sun Yanzi). 2000. "Black Sky" (Tian hei hei). In *Sun Yanzi SUN YAN-ZI* (Sun Yanzi SUN YAN-ZI). Taipei: Warner Music Taiwan.

———. 2002. "Olive Tree" (Ganlanshu). In *Start Anthology* (*Start Zixuanji*). Taipei: Warner Music.

———. 2003. "I'm Not Sad" (Wo bu nanguo). In *To Be Continued* (*Wei wancheng*). Taipei: Warner Music Taiwan.

———. 2003. "To Be Continued" (Wei wancheng). In *To Be Continued* (*Wei wancheng*). Taipei: Warner Music Taiwan.

Tao, David (Taozhe). 2002. "This Evening's News" (Jintian wanjian xinwen). In *Black Tangerine* (*Heisi liuding*). Taipei: Quanyuan Association.

———. 2002. "Angel." In *Black Tangerine* (*Heisi liuding*). Taipei: Quanyuan Association.

———. 2002. "Lullaby." In *Black Tangerine* (*Heisi liuding*). Taipei: Quanyuan Association.

———. 2002. "My Anata." In *Black Tangerine* (*Heisi liuding*). Taipei: Quanyuan Association.

Wawa. 1995. "Wanderer Without a Destination" (Meiyou zhongdian de liulang). In *Wanderer Without a Destination* (*Meiyou zhongdian de liulang*). Taipei: Rock Records.

Wong, Faye (Wang Fei). 1994. "Struggle to be Free" (Zhengtuo). In *Sky* (*Tiankong*). Hong Kong: Cinepoly/ Linfair Records Limited.

Zhang Qingfang. 1992. "Men's Talk." In *Rays of Light* (*Guangmang*). Taipei: Dianjiang Records.

Bibliography

Adams, Douglas. 1986. *The Ultimate Hitchhiker's Guide*. New York: Wings Books.

Adorno, Theodor W. [1941] 2000. "On Popular Music." In *On Record: Rock, Pop, and the Written Word*, ed. Simon Frith and Andrew Goodwin, 301–314. New York: Routledge.

Adrian, Bonnie. 2003. *Framing the Bride: Globalizing Beauty and Romance in Taiwan's Bridal Industry*. Berkeley: University of California Press.

Ahern (Martin), Emily. 1975. "The Power and Pollution of Chinese Women." In *Women in Chinese Society*, ed. Margery Wolf and Roxanne Witke, 193–214. Stanford, Calif.: Stanford University Press.

Allen, Robert C. 2001. "On Reading Soaps: A Semiotic Primer." In *Popular Culture: Production and Consumption*, 234–242. Oxford: Blackwell Publishers.

Andrews, Julia F., and Kuiyi Shen. 2002. "The New Chinese Woman and Lifestyle Magazines in the Late 1990s." In *Popular China: Unofficial Culture in a Globalizing Society*, ed. Richard P. Madsen, Perry Link, and Paul G. Pickowicz, 137–162. New York: Rowman & Littlefield Publishers, Inc.

Aoyagi, Hiroshi. 2000. "Pop Idols and the Asian Identity." In *Japan Pop! Inside the World of Japanese Popular Culture*, ed. Timothy J. Craig, 309–326. Armonk, N.Y.: M. E. Sharpe.

Appadurai, Arjun. 1996. *Modernity at Large: Cultural Dimensions of Globalization*. Minneapolis: University of Minnesota Press.

Asia Weekly. 2001. "Piracy Is Killing Taiwan's Music Circles" (Daoban shasi Taiwan yuetuan). *Asia Weekly Special Report* (*Zhoukan zhuanti baogao*). March 26–April 1: 46–49.

Atkins, E. Taylor. 2000. "Can Japanese Sing the Blues? 'Japanese Jazz' and the Problem of Authenticity." In *Japan Pop! Inside the World of Japanese Popular Culture*, ed. Timothy J. Craig, 27–59. Armonk, N.Y.: M. E. Sharpe.

———. 2001. *Blue Nippon: Authenticating Jazz in Japan*. Durham, N.C.: Duke University Press.

Baranovitch, Nimrod. 2003. *China's New Voices: Popular Music, Ethnicity, Gender, and Politics, 1978–1997*. Berkeley: University of California Press.

Barmé, Geremie. 1987. "Revolutionary Opera Arias Sung to a New Disco Beat." *The Far Eastern Economic Review* (December 26), 36–38.

Becker, Howard S. 2001. "Art as Collective Action." In *Popular Culture: Production and Consumption*, ed. C. Lee Harrington and Denise D. Bielby, 67–79. Oxford: Blackwell Publishers.

Bellah, Robert N., Richard Madsen, William M. Sullivan, Ann Swidler, and Steven M. Tipton. [1985] 1996. *Habits of the Heart: Individualism and Commitment in American Life*. Berkeley: University of California Press.

Benjamin, Walter. [1955] 1969. *Illuminations*. New York: Schocken Books.

Bennett, Andy. 2000. *Popular Music and Youth Culture: Music, Identity and Place*. New York: Palgrave.

Bhabha, Homi K. 1994. *The Location of Culture*. New York: Routledge.

Billboard.biz. 2005. "US Pop Charts." www.billboard.biz/bb/biz/yarendcharts/2005/tlptitl .jsp.

Blum, Susan D. 2001. *Portraits of "Primitives": Ordering Human Kinds in the Chinese Nation*. New York: Rowman & Littlefield Publishers, Inc.

Bordo, Susan. 1993. "Reading the Male Body." *Michigan Quarterly Review* 32(4): 696–737.

Boretz, Avron. 2004. "Carousing and Masculinity: The Cultural Production of Gender in Taiwan." In *Women in the New Taiwan: Gender Roles and Gender Consciousness in a Changing Society*, ed. Catherine Farris, Anru Lee, and Murray Rubinstein, 171–198. New York: M. E. Sharpe.

Brace, Tim. 1991. "Popular Music in Contemporary Beijing: Modernism and Cultural Identity." *Asian Music* 22(2): 43–66.

———. 1992. "Modernization and Music in Contemporary China: Crisis, Identity, and the Politics of Style." PhD dissertation, University of Texas.

Brace, Tim, and Paul Freidlander. 1992. "Rock and Roll on the New Long March: Popular Music, Cultural Identity, and Political Opposition in the People's Republic of China." In *Rockin' the Boat: Mass Music and Mass Movements*, ed. Reebee Garofalo, 115–128. Boston: South End Press.

Brenner, Suzanne. 1998. *The Domestication of Desire: Women, Wealth, and Modernity in Java*. Princeton, N.J.: Princeton University Press.

Brownell, Susan. 1995. *Training the Body for China: Sports in the Moral Order of the People's Republic*. Chicago: University of Chicago Press.

Burpee, Geoff, and Paul Mooney. 1997. "Sticky Contracts and Slim Margins Complicate Labels' Star-Search Inside the World's Biggest Market." *Billboard* 109(9): APQ2–APQ4.

Buxton, David. [1983] 2000. "Rock Music, the Star System, and the Rise of Consumerism." In *On Record: Rock, Pop, and the Written Word*, ed. Simon Frith and Andrew Goodwin, 427–440. New York: Routledge.

Cawelti, John G. 2001. "The Concept of Formula in the Study of Popular Culture." In *Popular Culture: Production and Consumption*, ed. C. Lee Harrington and Denise D. Bielby, 203–209. Oxford: Blackwell Publishers.

Ceng, Daxing. 1999. *Hero Worship and the Worship of Beautiful Women: Popular Music and the Culture of Fascination* (*Yingxiong chongbai yu meiren chongbai: liuxing gequ de wenhua meili*). Beijing: China United Culture Publishing.

Ceng, Huizhao. 1997. *Social Changes Reflected in the Verses of Popular Music in Taiwan: 1945-1995 (You liuxing yinyue de geci yanbian lai kan Taiwan de shehui bianqian: 1945-1995)*. Taipei: Wunan Library Publishing Company.

———. 1998 [2000] *Looking at Taiwan's Society through Taiwan's Pop Songs (Cong liuxing gechu kan Taiwan shehui)*. Taipei: Guiguan Books (Guiguan tushu).

Ceng, Wenzhi, and Liu Lingjun. 1997. "A Report on a Survey on Teenagers' Views and Attitudes Regarding Idols, Popular Music, and Slang" (Qingshaonian dui ouxiang, liuxing gequ, liuxing yongqu, zhi kanfa yu taidu diaocha baogao). *Journal of Student Counseling (Xuesheng fudao)* 41: 145-148.

Chan, Stephen C. K. (Chen Qingqiao), ed. 1997. *The Practice of Affect: Studies in Hong Kong Popular Song Lyrics (Qingan de shijian: Xianggang liuxing ge yanjiu)*. Edited by Stephen C. K. Chan (Chen Qingqiao). Hong Kong: Oxford University Press.

Chang, Shih-lun. 2007a. "The Future of Taiwanese Pop." Translated by Jonathan Barnard. *Taiwan Panorama* 32(1): 6-15.

———. 2007b. "Live Music Blossoms from the Grassroots." Translated by Geof Aberhart. *Taiwan Panorama* 32(1): 28-35.

———. 1997c. "In Praise of Youth—Sodagreen." Translated by Phil Newell. *Taiwan Panorama* 32(1): 26-27.

Chen, Huiling. 2002. "Research on Teenage Girls' Popular Music Bands: Image, Body Culture, and Carnal Desire" (Qingshaonü liuxingyinyue tuanti zhi yanjiu: xingxiang, shenti wenhua yu qingyu liudong). MA thesis. Furen University, Taipei.

Chen, Qianjun. 1997. "Lovers' Prattle and the Fashionable: A Deep Reading of Hong Kong's Popular Music and Culture." In *The Practice of Affect: Studies in Hong Kong Popular Song Lyrics (Qinggan de shijian: Xianggang liuxing de yanjiu)*, ed. Stephen C. K. Chan, 25-44. Hong Kong: Oxford University Press.

Chen Wanyi. 1996. "A Discussion of the Sorrowful [Ethos] of Taiwan's Literature (Lun Taiwan wenxue de 'beiqing')." In *A Collection of Taiwan's Theses in the Last One Hundred Years (Taiwan jin bai nian shi lunwen ji)*, ed. Zhang Yanxian, et al., 95-103. Taipei: Wuzhi Books Company.

Chen, Yanbing. 2000. *Love Is Like a Love Song: Love Strategies in Popular Music (Ai ru qingge: liuxing gequ de aiqing gonglue)*. Guangzhou: Southern Daily Publishing House.

Chen, Yuxiu. 1996. *Music Taiwan (Yinyue Taiwan)*. Taipei: National Library Publishing Catalogue Materials (Guojia tushuguan chubanpin yuxing pianmu ziliao).

———. 1998. *One Hundred Years of Taiwan's Music Pictorial History (Bainian Taiwan yinyue tuxiang yinyue tuxiang xunli)*. Taipei: Times Cultural Publishers.

Ching, Leo. 1995. "Imaginings in the Empire of the Sun: Japanese Mass Culture in Asia." In *Asia/Pacific as Space of Cultural Production*, ed. Rob Wilson and Arif Dirlik, 262-283. Durham, N.C.: Duke University Press.

———. 2001. "Globalizing the Regional, Regionalizing the Global: Mass Culture and Asianism in the Age of Late Capital." In *Globalization*, ed. Arjun Appadurai, 279-306. Durham, N.C.: Duke University Press.

Chow, Rey. 1991. *Women and Chinese Modernity: The Politics of Reading Between the West and East*. Minneapolis: University of Minnesota Press.

Chun, Allen. 2004. "World Music, Cultural Heteroglossia and Indigenous Capital: Overlapping Frequencies in the Emergence of Cosmopolitanism in Taiwan." In *Refashioning Pop Music in Asia: Cosmopolitan Flows, Political Tempos, and Aesthetic Industries*, ed. Allen Chun, Ned Rossiter, and Brian Shoesmith, 49–60. London: Taylor & Francis Inc.

Chun, Allen, and Ned Rossiter. 2004. "Introduction: Cultural Imaginaries, Musical Communities, Reflexive Practices." In *Refashioning Pop Music in Asia: Cosmopolitan Flows, Political Tempos, and Aesthetic Industries*, ed. Allen Chun, Ned Rossiter, and Brian Shoesmith, 1–14. London: Taylor & Francis Inc.

Chung, Oscar. 2005. "The Stars of East Asia Rising: Popular at Home and Across East Asia, Taiwanese Entertainers are Aiming High." *Taiwan Review* (October), 4–9.

Condry, Ian. 2001. "Japanese Hip-Hop and the Globalization of Popular Culture." In *Urban Life: Readings in the Anthropology of the City*, ed. George Gmelch and Walter Zenner, 357–387. Prospect Heights, Ill.: Waveland Press.

———. 2006. *Hip-Hop Japan: Rap and the Paths of Cultural Globalization*. Durham, N.C.: Duke University Press.

de Kloet, Jeroen. 2000. "'Let Him Fucking See the Green Smoke Beneath my Groin': The Mythology of Chinese Rock." In *Postmodernism and China*, ed. Arlif Dirlik and Zhang Xudong, 239–274. Durham, N.C.: Duke University Press.

———. 2001. *Red Sonic Trajectories: Popular Music and Youth in Urban China*. Amsterdam: Academisch Proefschrift.

———. 2003. "Notes on the Opaque Seduction of (Canto)pop: Sonic Imaginations." *IIAS Newsletter* 32: 25.

———. 2005a. "Authenticating Geographies and Temporalities: Representations of Chinese Rock in China." *Visual Anthropology* 18: 229–255.

———. 2005b. "Popular Music and Youth in Urban China—The *Dakou* Generation." *The China Quarterly* 183: 609–626.

———. 2005c. "Sonic Sturdiness: The Globalization of 'Chinese' Rock and Pop." *Critical Studies in Media Communication* 22(4): 321–338.

De Launey, Guy. 1995. "Western Pop Music in the Japanese Market." *Popular Music* 14(2): 203–225.

De Saint-Exupéry, Antoine. [1943]. *The Little Prince*. Translated by Katherine Woods. New York: Hartcourt, Brace & World.

Di Genova, Trista. 2005. "We Pop the Question to Taiwan's 'Young Heavenly King.'" *Taipei Times* (November 6), 18.

Dickens, Charles. [1861] 1994. *Great Expectations*. New York: Penguin Books.

Dikötter, Frank. 1995. *Sex, Culture, and Modernity in China: Medical Science and the Construction of Sexual Identities in the Early Republican Period*. London: Hurst & Company.

———. 1997. "Racial Discourse in China: Continuities and Permutations." In *The Construction of Racial Identities in China and Japan*, ed. Frank Dikötter, 12–33. Honolulu: University of Hawai'i Press.

Drake, Kate. 2003. "Cool Jay." *Time Asia* 61(8) (March 3): 75–86.

Drew, Rob. 2001. *Karaoke Nights: An Ethnographic Rhapsody*. Walnut Creek, Calif.: Alta Mira Press.

Dujunco, Mercedes M. 2002. "Hybridity and Disjuncture in Mainland Chinese Popular Music." In *Global Goes Local: Popular Culture in Asia*, ed. Timothy J. Craig and Richard King, 25–39. Vancouver: UBC Press.

Dyer, Richard. [1979] 2000. "In Defense of Disco." In *On Record: Rock, Pop, and the Written Word*, ed. Simon Frith and Andrew Goodwin, 410–418. New York: Routledge.

Efird, Robert. 2001. "Rock in a Hard Place: Music and the Market in Nineties Beijing." In *China Urban: Ethnographies of Contemporary China*, ed. Nancy N. Chen, Constance D. Clark, Suzanne Z. Gottschang, and Lyn Jeffery, 67–86. Durham, N.C.: Duke University Press.

ESWN, Culture Blog. 2006. "People Are Foolish, the Money Is Abundant, Come Quickly" (Ren sha, qian duo, su lai). http://lydon.yculblog.com/post.1177771.html.

Evans, Harriet. 1997. *Women and Sexuality in China: Dominant Discourses of Female Sexuality and Gender Since 1949*. Cambridge: Polity Press.

Ewen, Stuart. [1984] 1999. *All Consuming Images: The Politics of Style in Contemporary Culture*. New York: Basic Books.

Farrer, James. 2002. *Opening Up: Youth Sex Culture and Market Reform in Shanghai*. Chicago: University of Chicago Press.

Fiske, John. 1987. *Television Culture*. New York: Routledge.

———. 2001. "Intertextuality." In *Popular Culture: Production and Consumption*, ed. C. Lee Harrington and Denise D. Bielby, 219–233. Oxford: Blackwell Publishers.

Friedberg, Harris. 2001. "'Hang Up My Rock and Roll Shoes': The Cultural Production of Rock and Roll." In *Popular Culture: Production and Consumption*, ed. C. Lee Harrington and Denise D. Bielby, 154–164. Oxford: Blackwell Publishers.

Frith, Simon. 1988. *Music for Pleasure: Essays in the Sociology of Pop*. New York: Routledge.

———. 1996. *Performing Rites: On the Value of Popular Music*. Cambridge, Mass.: Harvard University Press.

Fu, Poshek. 1993. *Passivity, Resistance, and Collaboration: Intellectual Choices in Occupied Shanghai*. Stanford, Calif.: Stanford University Press.

———. 2003. *Between Shanghai and Hong Kong: The Politics of Chinese Cinemas*. Stanford, Calif.: Stanford University Press.

Fung, Anthony, and Michael Curtin. 2002. "The Anomalies of Being Faye (Wong): Gender Politics in Chinese Popular Music." *International Journal of Cultural Studies* 5(3): 263–290.

Garratt, Sheryl. [1984] 2000. "Teenage Dreams." In *On Record: Rock, Pop, and the Written Word*, ed. Simon Frith and Andrew Goodwin, 399–409. New York: Routledge.

Geertz, Clifford. 1973. *The Interpretation of Cultures*. New York: Basic Books.

Gerth, Karl. 2003. *China Made: Consumer Culture and the Creation of the Nation*. Cambridge, Mass.: Harvard University Press.

———. Forthcoming. *Chinese Consumerism in Modern Times*. Cambridge: Cambridge University Press.

G-Music. 2006. "G-music Billboard Chart Based on Sales from 2/3/06–2/9/06: A Combination of Rose Records (Meigui changpian), Dazhong Records (Dazhong changpian), and G-music." www.g-music.com.tw/GMusicBillboard1.aspx.

Gold, Thomas B. 1993. "Go With Your Feelings: Hong Kong and Taiwan Popular Culture in Greater China." *The China Quarterly* 136: 907–925.

Golden, Arthur. 2001. *Memoirs of a Geisha (Yi ge yiji de huiyi)*. Chinese translation by Lin Yurong. Taipei: Xidai Book Company Ltd.

Goodwin, Andrew. [1988] 2000. "Sample and Hold: Pop Music in the Digital Age of Reproduction." In *On Record: Rock, Pop, and the Written Word*, ed. Simon Frith and Andrew Goodwin, 258–273. New York: Routledge.

———. 1992. "Rationalization and Democratization in the New Technologies of Popular Music." In *Popular Music and Communication*, ed. James Lull, 75–100. Newbury Park, Calif.: Sage Publications.

Guy, Nancy. 2001. "How Does 'Made in Taiwan' Sound? Popular Music and Strategizing the Sounds of a Multicultural Nation." *Perfect Beat* 5(3): 1–17.

———. 2002a. "'Republic of China National Anthem' on Taiwan: One Anthem, One Performance, Multiple Realities." *Ethnomusicology* 46(1): 96–119.

———. 2002b. "Trafficking in Taiwan Aboriginal Voices." In *Handle with Care: Ownership and Control of Ethnographic Materials*, ed. Sjoerd R. Jaarsma. Pittsburgh: University of Pittsburgh Press.

Habermas, Jürgen. 1989. *The Structural Transformation of the Public Sphere: An Inquiry into a Category of Bourgeois Society*. Cambridge, Mass.: MIT Press.

Hanser, Amy. 2002. "The Chinese Enterprising Self: Young, Educated Urbanites and the Search for Work." In *Popular China: Unofficial Culture in a Globalizing Society*, ed. Perry Link, Richard P. Madsen, and Paul G. Pickowicz, 189–206. New York: Rowman & Littlefield Publishers.

Harrell, Steven. 1994. "Playing in the Valley: A Metonym of Modernization in Taiwan." In *Cultural Change in Postwar Taiwan*, ed. Huang Chun-chieh, 161–183. Boulder, Colo.: Westview Press.

Hebdige, Dick. 1987. *Cut 'N' Mix: Culture, Identity and Caribbean Music*. New York: Routledge.

———. [1979] 1991. *Subculture: The Meaning of Style*. New York: Routledge Press.

Henderson, David. 1996. "Emotion and Devotion, Lingering and Longing in Some Nepali Songs." *Ethnomusicology* 40(3): 440–468.

Hennion, Antoine. 1983. "The Production of Success: An Anti-Musicology of the Pop Song." *Popular Music* 3(3): 159–193.

Hermalin, Albert I., Paul K. C. Liu, and Deborah S. Freeman. 1994. "The Social and Economic Transformation of Taiwan." In *Social Change and the Family in Taiwan*, ed. Arland Thornton and Hui-Sheng Lin, 49–87. Chicago: University of Chicago Press.

Ho, Josephine (He Chunrui). 1994. "The Cultural Logic of Capital: The Case of McDonaldization in Taiwan" (Taiwan de maidanglaohua—kuaguofuwuye ziben de wenhua luoji). *A Radical Quarterly in Social Studies* (*Taiwan shehui yanjiu jikan*) 16: 1–20.

Ho, Wai-Chung. 2000. "The Political Meaning of Hong Kong Popular Music: A Review of Sociopolitical Relations between Hong Kong and the People's Republic of China since the 1980s." *Popular Music* 19(3): 341–353.

Hobsbawm, Eric. 1997a. "Introduction: Inventing Traditions." In *The Invention of Tradition*, ed. Eric Hobsbawm and Terence Ranger, 1–14. New York: Cambridge University Press.

———. 1997b. "Mass-Producing Traditions: Europe 1870–1914." In *The Invention of Tradition*, ed. Eric Hobsbawm and Terence Ranger, 263–308. New York: Cambridge University Press.

Honig, Emily, and Gail Hershatter. 1988. *Personal Voices: Chinese Women in the 1980s*. Stanford, Calif.: Stanford University Press.

Hooper, Beverley. 1994. "From Mao to Madonna: Sources on Contemporary Chinese Culture." *Southeast Asian Journal of Social Science* 22: 161–169.

Hou, Hsiao-hsien, dir. 2005. *Three Times*. Taipei: IFC.

Huang, Hao. 2001. "*Yaogun Yinyue*: Rethinking Mainland Chinese Rock'n'roll." *Popular Music* 20(1): 1–11.

———. 2003. "Voices from Chinese Rock, Past and Present Tense: Social Commentary and Construction of Identity in *Yaogun Yinyue*, from Tiananmen to the Present." *Popular Music and Society* 26(2): 183–202.

Huang Shusen. 2000. "Foreword." In Chen Yangbing, *Love Is Like a Love Song: Love Strategies in Popular Music* (*Ai ru qingge: liuxinggechu de aiqing gonglue*). Guangzhou: Southern Daily Publishers (*nanfang ribao chubanshi*), vi.

Hyde, Sandra Teresa. 2001. "Sex Tourism Practices on the Periphery: Eroticizing Ethnicity and Pathologizing Sex on the Langcang." In *China Urban: Ethnographies of Contemporary China*, ed. Nancy N. Chen, Constance D. Clark, Suzanne Z. Gottschang, and Lyn Jeffery, 143–162. Durham, N.C.: Duke University Press.

Ivory, James, dir. 2005. *The White Countess*. Los Angeles: Sony Pictures.

Ivy, Marilyn. 1995. *Discourses of the Vanishing. Modernity, Phantasm, Japan*. Chicago: University of Chicago Press.

Iwabuchi, Koichi. 1998. "Japanese Culture in Taiwan: The Odor of Globalization, Localization, and Modernity" (Riben wenhua zai Taiwan: quan qiu bentuhua yu xiandaixing de 'fangxiang'). *Modern Times Periodical* (*Dangdai qikan*) 125: 14–39.

2000. "To Globalize, Regionalize or Localize Us, That Is the Question: Japan's Response to Media Globalization." In *The New Communication Landscape: Demystifying Media Globalization*, ed. George Wang, Jan Seruges, and Anura Goonase, 142–159. New York: Routledge.

———. 2002. *Recentering Globalization: Popular Culture and Japanese Transnationalism*. Durham, N.C.: Duke University Press.

Jian, Weisi, and Guo Zhendi, dir. 2004. "Viva Tonal!—The Dance Age" (Tiaowu Shidai). Taipei: Taiwan Communications Science Company, Ltd.

Jiang Yizhi. 2006. "In Taiwan's Three Largest Urban Districts There Are 1.7 Million Lonely

Hearts Waiting for Happiness" (Taiwan san da bu hui chu—107 wan jimouxin dang-dai xinfu). *Yuanjian Magazine* (*Yuanjian zazhi*), April 10.

Johnson, Kay Ann. [1983] 1985. *Women, the Family and Peasant Revolution in China*. Chicago: The University of Chicago Press.

Jones, Andrew F. 1992. *Like a Knife: Ideology and Genre in Contemporary Chinese Popular Music*. Ithaca, N.Y.: Cornell University Press.

———. 1994. "The Politics of Popular Music in Post-Tiananmen China." In *Popular Protest and Political Culture in Modern China*, ed. Jeffrey N. Wasserstrom and Elizabeth J. Perry, 148–166. San Francisco: Westview Press.

———. 2001. *Yellow Music: Media Culture and Colonial Modernity in the Chinese Jazz Age*. Durham, N.C.: Duke University Press.

Jones, Stephen, and Stephen Hallet. 1994. "Swan Song: The Precarious Traditions of Chinese Music." In *World Music: The Rough Guide*, ed. Mark Ellingham, Simon Broughton, Dave Muddyman, and Richard Trillo, 452–457. New York: Rough Guides.

Ke, Yonghui. 1993. "Coming to Understand what Taiwan's Popular Music Says about Women" (Jiedu Taiwan liuxing yingue zhong de nüxing yihan). MA thesis, Zhengshi University, Taiwan.

Ke, Yonghui, and Jinhua Zhang. 1995. *Mass Media's Women, Women's Mass Media—Part One* (*Meiti de nüren, nüren de meiti—shang*). Taipei: Shuoren Publishing House, Ltd.

Kealy, Edward R. [1979] 2000. "From Craft to Art: The Case of Sound Mixers and Popular Music." In *On Record: Rock, Pop, and the Written Word*, ed. Simon Frith and Andrew Goodwin, 207–220. New York: Routledge.

Keane, Michael. 2002. "Television Drama in China: Engineering Souls for the Market." In *Global Goes Local: Popular Culture in Asia*, ed. Timothy J. Craig and Richard King, 120–137. Vancouver: USB Press.

Kelly, Bill. [1998] 2001. "Japan's Empty Orchestras: Echoes of Japanese Culture in the Performance of Karaoke." In *The Worlds of Japanese Popular Culture: Gender, Shifting Boundaries and Global Cultures*, ed. Dolores P. Martinez, 75–87. New York: Cambridge University Press.

Kondo, Dorinne K. 1990. *Crafting Selves: Power, Gender, and Discourses of Identity in a Japanese Workplace*. Chicago: The University of Chicago Press.

Kraus, Richard C. 1989. *Pianos and Politics in China: Middle-Class Ambitions and the Struggle over Western Music*. New York: Oxford University Press.

Lai, T. C., and Robert Mok. 1981. *Jade Flute: The Story of Chinese Music*. New York: Schocken Books.

Lau, Wai-keung, dir. 2002. *Infernal Affairs* (*Wu jian dao*). Hong Kong: Media Asia Films.

Lee, Ang, dir. 2007. *Lust, Caution* (*Si jie*). Los Angeles: Universal Studios.

Lee, Anru. 2004a. "Between Filial Daughter and Loyal Sister: Global Economy and Family Politics in Taiwan." In *Women in the New Taiwan: Gender Roles and Gender Consciousness in a Changing Society*, ed. Catherine Farris, Anru Lee, and Murray Rubinstein, 101–119. New York: M. E. Sharpe.

———. 2004b. *In the Name of Harmony and Prosperity: Labor and Gender Politics in Taiwan's Economic Restructuring*. New York: State University of New York Press.

Lee, Gregory B. 1995. "The 'East Is Red' Goes Pop: Commodification, Hybridity and Nationalism in Chinese Popular Song in its Televisual Performance." *Popular Music* 14(1): 95–110.

———. 1996. *Troubadours, Trumpeters, Troubled Makers: Lyricism, Nationalism, and Hybridity in China and its Others*. London: Hurst.

Lee, Leo Ou-fan. 1999. *Shanghai Modern: The Flowering of a New Urban Culture in China 1930–1945*. Cambridge, Mass.: Harvard University Press.

Lee, Vito. 2007a. "Hard Times Hit the Middle Class—A New Lesson in Capitalism for Taiwan?" Translated by Phil Newell. *Taiwan Panorama* 32(1): 76–85.

———. 2007b. "What Help for the New Poor?" *Taiwan Panorama* 32(1): 86–90.

Leng, Sui-jin. 1991. "The Shock of Hong Kong and Taiwan Popular Songs." Translated by Peter Rigs. *Popular Music and Society* 15(2): 23–32.

Levy, Richard. 2002. "Corruption in Popular Culture." In *Popular China: Unofficial Culture in a Globalizing Society*, ed. Perry Link, Richard P. Madsen, and Paul G. Pickowicz, 39–56. New York: Rowman & Littlefield Publishers.

Li, Luxin. 1993. *Popular Music: The Home of Youth of that Time* (*Liuxing gequ: dangdai qingnian de jiayuan*). Beijing: Huaxia Publishers.

Li, Siu-leung. 2003. *Cross-Dressing in Chinese Opera*. Hong Kong: Hong Kong University Press.

Liang, Hongbin. 2001. "Taiwan's Popular Music Culture from the Perspective of the Wild Popularity of Japan and the Popularity of Korea" (Cong hari feng yu hanliu tan Taiwan yinyue wenhua). *Publishing Almanac Editorial Board* (*Chuban nianjian bianji wei yuanhui*): 176–179. [Taipei] China Publishing Company ([Taipei] Zhongguo chuban gongsi).

Liew, Kai Khiun. 2003. "Limited Pidgin-type Patois? Policy, Language, Technology, Identity and the Experience of Canto-pop in Singapore." *Popular Music* 22(2): 217–233.

Lin, Hsin-Yi. 1989. Popular Music Industries Production and Marketing in Contemporary Taiwan: Production and Distribution. Institute of Information (*Dangdai Taiwan yinyue gongye chanxiao jiego fenxi*). MA thesis, Yuan-Ze University, Zhong Li, Taiwan.

Lipsitz, George. 1994. *Dangerous Crossroads: Popular Music, Postmodernism and the Poetics of Place*. New York: Verso Press.

———. 2001. "Diasporic Noise: History, Hip Hop, and the Post-colonial Politics of Sound." In *Popular Culture: Production and Consumption*, ed. C. Lee Harrington and Denise D. Bielby, 180–200. Oxford: Blackwell Publishers.

Liu, Honglin. 1999. "An Analysis of the Ways in Which Mandopop Serves as an Educational Tool about Dating" (Yi guoyu liuxing gequ jinxing liangxing yi jiaoxue zhe chengxiao fenxi). MA thesis, Donghua University, Taiwan.

Liu Huijun. 1992. "Who Is Deciding Conceptions of Women, and What Are These Concepts? From Urban Women's Songs Discussing Women's Music Practice" (Shei wei nüren dading sheme zhuyi? Cong dushi nüxingge tan nüxing yinyue shijian?). *Women's New Awareness* (*Funü xinzhi*) 1(1): 16–19.

Liu, Kedi, and Liang Junmei. 2003. *The Mortal Days—San Mao's Love Songs of Life*.

(*Hongchen suiyue—San Mao de shengming liange*). Taipei: Metropolitan Culture Enterprise Co. Ltd.

Liu, Xing. 1984. *The Origin and Development of Chinese Popular Music's Melodies (Zhongguo liuxing gequ yuanliu)*. Taipei: Government Information Office of Taiwan.

Lo, Kwai-cheung. 2001. "Transnationalization of the Local in Hong Kong Cinema of the 1990s." In *At Full Speed: Hong Kong Cinema in a Borderless World*, ed. Esther C. M. Yau, 261–276. Minneapolis: University of Minnesota Press.

Lu, Hanxiu. 2003. *The Sound of Love Songs (Gesheng lianqing)*. Taipei: United Articles.

Lü, Yuxiu. 2003. *A History of Taiwan's Music (Taiwan yinyueshi)*. Taipei: Wunan Book Publishing Company.

Lum, Casey Man Kong. 1998. "The Karaoke Dilemma: On the Interaction Between Collectivism and Individualism in the Karaoke Space." In *Karaoke Around the World: Global Technology, Local Singing*, ed. Tōru Mitsui and Shūhei Hosokawa, 166–177. New York: Routledge Press.

———. 1996. *In Search of a Voice: Karaoke and the Construction of Identity in Chinese America*. Mahwah, N.J.: Lawrence Erlbaum Associates.

Manuel, Peter. 1988. *Popular Musics of the Non-Western World*. New York: Oxford University Press.

Momphard, David. 2003. "Features: Brothers Gonna Work it Out." *Taipei Times* (November 1), 16.

Morris, Andrew D. 2002. "'I Believe You Can Fly': Basketball Culture in Postsocialist China." In *Popular China: Unofficial Culture in a Globalizing Society*, ed. Richard P. Madsen, Perry Link, and Paul G. Pickowicz, 9–38. New York: Rowman & Littlefield Publishers.

———. 2004a. "Baseball, History, the Local and the Global in Taiwan." In *The Minor Arts of Daily Life: Popular Culture in Taiwan*, ed. Andrew D. Morris, David K. Jordan, and Marc L. Moskowitz, 176–203. Honolulu: University of Hawai'i Press.

———. 2004b. *Marrow of the Nation: A History of Sport and Physical Culture in Republican China*. Berkeley: University of California Press.

Morrison, Toni. [1987] 1997. *Beloved*. New York: Vintage Press.

Moskowitz, Marc L. 2001. *The Haunting Fetus: Abortion, Sexuality, and the Spirit World in Taiwan*. Honolulu: University of Hawai'i Press.

———. 2004. "Yang-Sucking She-Demons: Penetration, Fear of Castration, and other Freudian Angst in Modern Chinese Cinema." In *The Minor Arts of Daily Life: Popular Culture in Modern Taiwan*, ed. Andrew D. Morris, David K. Jordan, and Marc L. Moskowitz, 204–217. Honolulu: University of Hawai'i Press.

———. 2007. "Failed Families and Quiet Individualism: Women's Strategies of Resistance in Urban Taiwan." *Journal of Archaeology and Anthropology* 67: 157–184.

———. 2008. "Multiple Virginity, Barbarian Prince Charmings, and Other Contested Realities in Taipei's Foreign Club Culture." *Sexualities* 11(3): 327–335.

Murakami, Haruki. [1980] 2002. *Coin Locker Babies*. Translated by Stephen Snyder. New York: Kodansha International.

Napier, Susan J. 2001. *Anime from Akira to Princess Mononoke: Experiencing Contemporary Japanese Animation*. New York: Palgrave.

Nonini, Donald, and Aihwa Ong. 1997. "Introduction." In *Ungrounded Empires: The Cultural Politics of Modern Chinese Transnationalism*, ed. Donald Nonini and Aihwa Ong, 3–33. New York: Routledge.

Oba, Junko. 2002. "To Fight the Losing War, to Remember the Lost War: The Changing Role of *Gunka*, Japanese War Songs." In *Global Goes Local: Popular Culture in Asia*, ed. Timothy J. Craig and Richard King, 225–245. Vancouver: USB Press.

Ogawa, Hiroshi. 1998. "The Effects of Karaoke on Music in Japan." In *Karaoke Around the World: Global Technology, Local Singing*, ed. Tōru Mitsui and Hosokawa Shūhei, 45–54. New York: Routledge Press.

———. 2004. "Japanese Popular Music in Hong Kong: What Does TK Present?" In *Refashioning Pop Music in Asia: Cosmopolitan Flows, Political Tempos, and Aesthetic Industries*, ed. Allen Chun, Ned Rossiter, and Brian Shoesmith, 144–156. London: Taylor & Francis Inc.

Ohnuki-Tierney, Emiko. 1997. "McDonald's in Japan: Changing Manners and Etiquette." In *Golden Arches East: McDonald's in East Asia*, ed. James L. Watson, 161–182. Stanford, Calif.: Stanford University Press.

Oku, Shinobu. 1998. "Karaoke and Middle-Aged and Older Women." In *Karaoke Around the World: Global Technology, Local Singing*, ed. Tōru Mitsui and Shūhei Hosokawa, 55–80. New York: Routledge Press.

Ong, Aihwa. 1999. *Flexible Citizenship: The Cultural Logics of Transnationality*. Durham, N.C.: Duke University Press.

Ōtake, Akiko, and Shūhei Hosokawa. 1998. "Karaoke in East Asia: Modernization, Japanization, or Asianization?" In *Karaoke Around the World: Global Technology, Local Singing*, ed. Tōru Mitsui, and Shūhei Hosokawa, 178–201. New York: Routledge Press.

Perris, Arnold. 1983. "Music as Propaganda: Art at the Command of Doctrine in the People's Republic of China." *Ethnomusicology* 17(1): 1–28.

Raz, Aviad E. 1999. *Riding the Black Ship: Japan and Tokyo Disneyland*. Cambridge, Mass.: Harvard University Press.

Reheja, Gloria G., and Ann G. Gold. 1994. *Listen to the Heron's Words: Reimagining Gender and Kinship in North India*. Berkeley: University of California Press.

Robinson, Deana Campbell, Elizabeth Buck, and Merlene Cuthbert. 1991. *Music at the Margins: Popular Music and Global Cultural Diversity*. London: Sage Publications.

Rosenberger, Nancy R. 2001. *Gambling with Virtue: Japanese Women and the Search for Self in a Changing Nation*. Honolulu: University of Hawai'i Press.

Rose Records. 2002. "Taiwan Top 20." www.roserecords.com.tw.

Said, Edward W. 1978. *Orientalism*. New York: Penguin.

Sangren, Steven P. 1993. "Female Gender in Chinese Religious Symbols: Kuan Yin, Ma Tsu, and the 'Eternal Mother.'" *Signs* 9(1): 4–25.

———. 1996. "Myths, Gods, and Family Relations." In *Unruly Gods: Divinity and Society in China*, ed. Meir Shahar and Robert P. Weller, 105–149. Honolulu: University of Hawai`i Press.

———. 2000. *Chinese Sociologics: An Anthropological Account of the Role of Alienation and Social Reproduction*. London: Athlone.

Sanjek, David. 2001. "'Don't Have to DK no More': Sampling and the 'Autonomous' Creator." In *Popular Culture: Production and Consumption*, ed. C. Lee Harrington and Denise D. Bielby, 243–256. Oxford: Blackwell Publishers.

Seaman, Gary. 1981. "The Sexual Politics of Karmic Retribution." In *The Anthropology of Taiwanese Society*, ed. Emily Martin Ahern and Hill Gates, 381–396. Stanford, Calif.: Stanford University Press.

Schein, Louisa. 2000. *Minority Rules: The Miao and the Feminine in China's Cultural Politics*. Durham, N.C.: Duke University Press.

Sharman, Jim, dir. 1975. *The Rocky Horror Picture Show*. Twentieth Century-Fox Film Corporation.

Shih Yun-ru (Shi Yunru). 2004. "From Beats to Entertainment: The Transformation of Production and Marketing in the Popular Music Industry" (You jiepai xuanlü dao yule shangpin: Taiwan liuxingyinyue chanye chanxiao jiegou zhuanbian yanjiu). MA thesis, Chiao Tung University, Xinju, Taiwan.

Shuker, Roy. 1994. *Understanding Popular Music*. New York: Routledge.

Silvio, Teri J. 1998. "Drag Melodrama/Feminine Sphere/Folk Television: Local Opera and Identity in Taiwan." PhD dissertation, University of Chicago.

Simon, Scott. 2003. *Sweet and Sour: Life Worlds of Taipei Women Entrepreneurs*. Lanham, Md.: Rowman & Littlefield.

Stacey, Judith. 1983. *Patriarchy and Socialist Revolution in China*. Berkeley: University of California Press.

Stanlaw, James. 1992. "'For Beautiful Human Life': The Use of English in Japan." In *Re-made in Japan: Everyday Life and Consumer Taste in a Changing Society*, ed. Joseph J. Tobin, 58–76. New Haven, Conn.: Yale University Press.

———. 2000. "Open Your File, Open Your Mind: Women, English, and Changing Roles and Voices in Japanese Pop Music." In *Japan Pop! Inside the World of Japanese Popular Culture*, ed. Timothy J. Craig, 75–100. New York: M. E. Sharpe.

Stokes, David. 2004. "Popping the Myth of Chinese Rock." In *Refashioning Pop Music in Asia: Cosmopolitan Flows, Political Tempos, and Aesthetic Industries*, ed. Allen Chun, Ned Rossiter, and Brian Shoesmith, 32–48. London: Taylor & Francis Inc.

Su, Zhensheng. 1999. "Conceptions of the Value of Love in Taiwan's Pop Music: 1989–1998" (Taiwan liuxing yinyue zhong de aiqing jiazhiguan: 1989–1998). MA thesis, Zhong Shan University, Taiwan.

Sugarman, Jane C. 1989. "The Nightingale and the Partridge: Singing and Gender among Prespa Albanians." *Ethnomusicology* 33(2): 191–215.

———. 1997. *Engendering Song: Singing and Subjectivity at Prespa Albanian Weddings*. Chicago: University of Chicago Press.

Taipei Times. 2006. "Taiwan Quick Take: Southerners Are More Lonely" (March 29), 3.

Taiwan's Executive Yuan CPC. 2006. Popular Culture Products Center (Liuxing wenhua chanye zhongxin). International Arts and Popular Music Center (Guoji yixhu). Executive Yuan Cultural Promotion Committee (Xingzhengyuan wenhua jianshe weiyuanhui).

Tanaka, Keiko. 1998. "Japanese Women's Magazines: The Language of Aspiration." In *The Worlds of Japanese Popular Culture: Gender, Shifting Boundaries and Global Cultures*, ed. Dolores P. Martinez, 110–132. New York: Cambridge University Press.

Tanizaki, Junichirō. [1928–1929] 2001. *Some Prefer Nettles*. Translated by Edward G. Seidensticker. New York: Tuttle Publishing.

Tansman, Alan M. 1996. "Mournful Tears and Sake: The Postwar Myth of Misora Hibari." In *Contemporary Japan and Popular Culture*, ed. John Wittier Treat, 103–133. Honolulu: University of Hawai`i Press.

Taussig, Michael T. 1993. *Mimesis and Alterity: A Particular History of the Senses*. New York: Routledge.

Taylor, Jeremy E. 2004. "Pop Music as Postcolonial Nostalgia in Taiwan." In *Refashioning Pop Music in Asia: Cosmopolitan Flows, Political Tempos, and Aesthetic Industries*, ed. Allen Chun, Ned Rossiter, and Brian Shoesmith, 173–182. London: Taylor & Francis.

Thompson, Eric C. 2002. "Rocking East and West: The USA in Malaysian Music" (an American Remix). In *Global Goes Local: Popular Culture in Asia*, ed. Timothy J. Craig and Richard King, 58–79. Vancouver: USB Press.

Treat, John Wittier. 1996. "Introduction: Japanese Studies into Cultural Studies." In *Contemporary Japan and Popular Culture*, ed. John Wittier Treat, 1–14. Honolulu: University of Hawai`i Press.

Tsai, Futuro (Cai Zhengliang), dir. 2005. *Amis Hip Hop (Amei xiha)*. Hsinju, Taiwan: Institute of Anthropology, National Tsing-Hwa University.

Tsai, Wen-ting. 2002a. "Taiwanese Pop Will Never Die." *Sinorama* 27(6): 6–19.

———. 2002b. "Taiwanese Popular Music's First Star—The Black Cat, Ai-ai." *Sinorama* 27(6): 20–22.

Twain, Mark. [1869] 1966. *The Innocents Abroad*. New York: Penguin Books.

van Gulik, Robert H. [1961] 1974. *Sexual Life in Ancient China: A Preliminary Survey of Chinese Sex and Society from 1500 B.C. until 1644 A.D.* Leiden: E. J. Brill.

Van Maanen, John. 1992. "Displacing Disney: Some Notes on the Flow of Culture." *Qualitative Sociology* 15(1): 5–35.

Wakeman, Frederic Jr. 1995. *Policing Shanghai 1927–1937*. Berkeley: University of California Press.

Wang, Georgette. 1986. "Popular Music in Taiwan." *Critical Studies in Mass Communication* 3(3): 366–368.

Watson, James L. 1997a. *Golden Arches East: McDonald's in East Asia*. Stanford, Calif.: Stanford University Press.

———. 1997b. "Introduction: Transnationalism, Localization, and Fast Foods in East Asia." In *Golden Arches East: McDonald's in East Asia*, ed. James L. Watson, 1–38. Stanford, Calif.: Stanford University Press.

———. 1997c. "McDonald's in Hong Kong: Consumerism, Dietary Change, and the Rise of a Children's Culture." In *Golden Arches East: McDonald's in East Asia*, ed. James L. Watson, 77–109. Stanford, Calif.: Stanford University Press.

———. 1998. "Living Ghosts: Long-Haired Destitutes in Colonial Hong Kong." In *Hair: Its Power and Meaning in Asian Cultures*, ed. A. Hiltebeitel and B. Miller, 177–194. Albany: State University of New York Press.

Wei, Hung-chin. 1992. "Cramming for Karaoke." Translated by Phil Newell. *Sinorama*: 38–41.

Weinstein, Deana. 1991. *Heavy Metal: A Cultural Sociology*. New York: Lexington Books.

Wells, Alan. 1997. "The International Music Business in Taiwan: The Cultural Transmission of Western and Chinese Music." *Media Asia* 24(4): 206–213.

White, Adam. 1998. "Majors' Designs on China Include Local Music." *Billboard* 110(25): 91.

Witzleben, Laurence J. 1999. "Cantopop and Mandopop in Pre-postcolonial Hong Kong: Identity Negotiations in the Performance of Anita Mui Yim-fong." *Popular Music* 18(2): 241–258.

Wolf, Margery. 1968. *The House of Lim: A Study of a Chinese Farm Family*. Englewood Cliffs, N.J.: Prentice Hall.

———. 1972. *Women and the Family in Rural Taiwan*. Stanford, Calif.: Stanford University Press.

———. 1975. "Women and Suicide in China." In *Women in Chinese Society*, ed. Margery Wolf and Roxanne Witke, 111–142. Stanford, Calif.: Stanford University Press.

Wong, Isabel K. F. 2002. "The Incantation of Shanghai: Singing a City into Existence." In *Global Goes Local: Popular Culture in Asia*, ed. Timothy J. Craig and Richard King, 246–264. Vancouver: UBC Press.

Wong, James. 1997. "Popular Music and Hong Kong Culture." In *Asian Music with Special Reference to China and India*, ed. Ching-Chih Liu, 95–110. Hong Kong: Music Symposia of 34th ICANAS.

Wong, Jiaming. 2003. "Taiwan's Popular Music Advances to Mainland China—New Developments and Predicaments for Popular Music on Both Sides of the Straights" (Taiwan liuxing yinyue qianjin dalu liang an liuxing yinyue de kunjing ji xinji). In *Publishing Almanac Editorial Board* (*Chuban nianjian bian ji wei yuanhui*), 152–157. Taipei: China Publishing Company.

Wong, Victor. 1998a. "Taiwan's Rock Divided into 5 Labels." *Billboard* 110(25): 65–67.

———. 1998b. "Taiwan Going Strong Despite Setbacks." *Billboard* 110(43): APQ1–APQ4.

———. 1998c. "The Year in Asia." *Billboard*. 110(52): YE26.

———. 1999. "Avex Launches Taiwan Subsidiary to Build Label's Local Profile." *Billboard* 111(9): 47–48.

Woolf, Virginia. [1928] 1993. *Orlando*. New York: Penguin Books.

Wu, David Y. H. 1997. "McDonald's in Taipei: Hamburgers, Betel Nuts, and National Identity." In *Golden Arches East: McDonald's in East Asia*, ed. James L. Watson, 110–135. Stanford, Calif.: Stanford University Press.

Wu, Jia-Yu. 1997. "Between Traditional Musical Practices and Contemporary Musical Life:

A Study of the Karaoke Phenomenon in Taiwan." PhD dissertation, University of California at Los Angeles.

Wu, Jing-jyi. [1985] 2001. *Shyness, Loneliness, and Love (Haixiu, jimo, ai)*. Taipei: Yuanliu Publishing House, Ltd.

Xiao, Pin, and Su Zhensheng. 2002. "Penetrating the Dense Fog of Blind Love: Unraveling the World of Love in Taiwan's Music—1989–1998" (Jiekai fenghuaxueyue de miwu: jiedu Taiwan liuxing yinyue zhong de aiqing shijie—1989–1998). *Journalism Studies (Xinwenxue yanjiu)* 17: 167–195.

Xu, Xiuhui. 2002. "Independent Report—Taiwan Music Dominates the World's Chinese Music Market" (Dujia baodao Taiwan yinyue chenba quanqiu huaren shichang). *Wealth (Caixun)* 246: 323–327.

Yang, Irene Fang-Chih. 1992. "The History of Popular Music in Taiwan." *Popular Music and Society* 18(3): 55–66.

———. 1993. "A Genre Analysis of Popular Music in Taiwan." *Popular Music and Society* 17(2): 83–112.

———. 1996. "Working Class Girls and Popular Music in Taiwan." *Jump Cut: A Review of Contemporary Media* 40: 74–84.

Yang, Mayfair Mei-hui. 1997. "Mass Media and Transnational Subjectivity in Shanghai: Notes on (Re)Cosmopolitianism in a Chinese Metropolis." In *Ungrounded Empires: The Cultural Politics of Modern Chinese Transnationalism*, ed. Aihwa Ong and Donald Macon Nonini, 287–319. New York: Routledge.

———. 2004. "Goddess across the Taiwan Straits: Matrifocal Ritual Space, Nation-State, and Satellite Television Footprints." *Public Culture* 16(2): 209–238.

Yano, Christine R. 2000. "The Marketing of Tears: Consuming Emotions in Japanese Popular Song." In *Japan Pop! Inside the World of Japanese Popular Culture*, ed. Timothy J. Craig, 60–74. Armonk, N.Y.: M. E. Sharpe.

———. 2003. *Tears of Longing: Nostalgia and the Nation in Japanese Popular Song*, Harvard East Asian Monographs. Cambridge, Mass.: Harvard University Press.

Ye, Longyan. 2001. *Thoughts on Taiwan's Records (Taiwan changpian xixiang qi)*. Taipei: Boyang Culture Industry Company, Ltd.

Yeh, Yueh-yu. 1995. "A National Score: Popular Music and Taiwanese Cinema." PhD dissertation, University of Southern California.

Yu, Shuenn-Der. 2004. "Hot and Noisy: Taiwan's Night Market Culture." In *The Minor Arts of Daily Life: Popular Culture in Taiwan*, ed. Andrew D. Morris, David K. Jordan, and Marc L. Moskowitz, 129–149. Honolulu: University of Hawai`i Press.

Zhang, Chuanwei. 2003. *Who Is Singing Their Own Song Over There: A History of Taiwan's Contemporary Folk Song Movement (Shei zai nabian chang ziji de ge: Taiwan xiandai minge yundong shi)*. Taipei: Rock Publications Co. Ltd.

Zhang, Meijun. 1997. "A Return Journey to Hong Kong's 1980s Nationalist Sentiment in Pop Music Melodies" (Huigui zhi lu bashi niandai yilai Xianggang liuxing chuzhong de jia qing). In *The Practice of Affect: Studies in Hong Kong Popular Song Lyrics (Qinggan de shijian: Xianggang liuxing ge yanjiu)*, ed. Stephen C. K. Chan (Chen Qingqiao), 45–74. Hong Kong: Oxford University Press.

Zhang, Xiaohong. 1991. "Red Man, Green Woman: Love Songs, Popular Culture, and the Subversion of Gender" (Hong nan, lunü: qingge, liuxing wenhua yu xinbie dianfu). *United Literature (Lianhe wenxue)* 7(10): 85–89.

Zhang, Yimou, dir. 1989. *Red Sorghum.* Xi'an, PRC: Xi'an Film Studio.

———, dir. 2007. *Curse of the Golden Flower.* Sony Pictures.

Zhao, Yuezhi. 2002. "The Rich, the Laid-off, and the Criminal in Tabloid Tales Read All about It!" In *Popular China: Unofficial Culture in a Globalizing Society,* ed. Perry Link, Richard P. Madsen, and Paul G. Pickowicz, 111–136. New York: Rowman & Littlefield Publishers.

Zheng, Jianli, Zhou Tingyu, and Wu Xiaowen. 2004. *Garden of Sounds: MTV's Spatial Meaning (Huayuan shengyin: MTV de yiyi kongjian).* Beijing: Central Compilation Publishing House.

Zheng, Shuyi. 1992. "Taiwan's Popular Music and Mass Media Culture: 1982–1991" (Taiwan liuxing yinyue yu dazhong wenhua: 1982 nian). MA thesis, Furen University, Taiwan.

Zheng, Su. 1997. "Female Heroes and Moonish Lovers: Women's Paradoxical Identities in Modern Chinese Songs." *Journal of Women's History* 8(4): 91–125.

Zhou, Qianyi. 1998. "From Faye Wong to Fans—Popular Music, Idol Worship, Androgyny, the Formation of the Subjectivity of Gender" (Cong Wang Fei dao feimi—liuxing yinyue yuxiang chongbai zhongxingbie zhuti de bocheng). *News Research (Xinwenxue yanjiu)* 56: 105–134.

Zhou, Zhaoping. 1997. "Research on Taiwan's Mandopop Recording Industry: A Comparative Case Study for Rock Records International and Sony Records" (Taiwan changpian gongsi huayu liuxinggequ chanzhi yanjiu: gunshi guoji yu xinli yinyue de gean bijiao). MA thesis, Zhongshan University, Taiwan.

Zhu, Yaowei. 2000. *Glorious Days: A Study of Pop Groups in Hong Kong: 1984–1990 (Guanghui suiyue: Xianggang liuxing yuedui zuhe yanjiu: 1984–1990).* Hong Kong: Huizhi Publishing.

Index

About the Author

MARC L. MOSKOWITZ is an associate professor in the Department of Anthropology at the University of South Carolina and the Visual Anthropology Review Editor for the *American Anthropologist*. He is a recipient of the Chiang Ching-Kuo, Fulbright, and Fulbright-Hays awards. He is the author of *The Haunting Fetus: Abortion, Sexuality, and the Spirit World in Taiwan* (2001) and co-editor of *The Minor Arts of Daily Life: Popular Culture in Taiwan* (2004). He has also published in a range of journals in the United States and Taiwan including *The China Quarterly, Popular Music,* and *Sexualities.*

Production Notes for Moskowitz | *Cries of Joy, Songs of Sorrow*

Cover design by Julie Matsuo-Chun

Composition by Santos Barbasa Jr.

Text design by University of Hawai'i Press Production Department
with display type in Gill Sans and text type in Minion

Printing and binding by The Maple-Vail Book Manufacturing Group

Printed on 60 lb. Maple Recycled Opaque, 408 ppi.